THE TRUE SELF

CONSCIOUS LIVING - UNLOCK THE JOY IN YOU

Lokesh (Loki) Babu

Copyright © 2024 (Lokesh (Loki) Babu)
All rights reserved worldwide.

No part of the book may be copied or changed in any format, sold, or used in a way other than what is outlined in this book, under any circumstances, without the prior written permission of the publisher.

Inspiring Publishers
P.O. Box 159, Calwell, ACT Australia 2905
Email: publishaspg@gmail.com
http://www.inspiringpublishers.com

 A catalogue record for this book is available from the National Library of Australia

National Library of Australia The Prepublication Data Service

Author: Lokesh (Loki) Babu
Title: The True Self: Conscious Living - Unlock the joy in you
Genre: Nonfiction

Paperback ISBN: 978-1-923250-20-8
ePub2 ISBN: 978-1-923250-21-5
PDF eBook ISBN: 978-1-923250-22-2

ACKNOWLEDGEMENTS

I am thankful for the support of my family & friends. They are a part of my life and my journey. I am particularly grateful to Josipa for her support in the last twelve years of my self-transformation to who I am today. I express gratitude to the universe for the joy and love it gave me to experience, and the life lessons I learnt.

Thank you to my late father and late mother for giving me this beautiful life. My gratitude to everyone who directly or indirectly contributed to this book and or has been in my journey.

I want to acknowledge life itself
for all the opportunities and experiences.

This book is dedicated to
All Seekers of Truth and Wisdom.

CONTENTS

Preface vii

1. Separation, Inequality, and the Drive to Search for Truth 1
2. Finding Clarity, and the Strength to Follow your Heart 64
3. From Separation to Union 103
4. Acceptance, Silence and Inner Peace 137
5. Witnessing 163

About the Author 195

Bibliography 196

PREFACE

One Truth, Many Paths

Every journey, every path, begins with one step. I took mine in Varanasi, in 2015.

The oldest living city in the world and India's spiritual heart, Varanasi lies on the banks of the Ganges, whose sacred waters flow down from the Himalayas. Mark Twain described the city as 'older than history, older than tradition, older even than legend, and looks twice as old as all of them put together'. I was on my way out of the city, heading back to Mumbai when I paused to buy a few second-hand books from a street seller. These were: the complete works of Rabindranath Tagore, an Indian poet, writer, philosopher, and painter who won the Nobel prize for literature in 1913 and composed India's national anthem; Plato's *The Republic*; and *The Histories* by Herodotus, often referred to as the father of history.

I hadn't gone looking for these books, I was just in the right place to find them, both in the world and in myself. I had been introduced to Rumi, 13th-century Persian poet, scholar, and Sufi mystic, in Istanbul three years earlier, and was beginning to ask the questions I seek to answer in *The True Self*: Who am I? What is the purpose of life? What is its meaning? But it wasn't until I held these cheaply bought books in my hands, and with the Himalayas at my back of my mind, that I began the practice that has led me here. I read, I underlined, and I wrote my thoughts in those books. Suddenly, nothing else seemed to matter. Time no longer existed. While seeking truth from these ancient teachings, I felt an effortless flow of energy, let go of my own limited identity and connected with the universe.

Ever since that simple-seeming choice, made on the outskirts of Varanasi, I have sought wisdom from scholars, philosophers, and yogis, from the past and the present, belonging to a myriad of cultures from across the world, all to understand my True Self. As I did so, I made notes and began to incorporate what I had learned in my day-to-day life.

Most of the commentary in this book was written in my home country of Australia, on the train journey I took every weekend to visit my daughter. Far from Varanasi, no Himalayas as my backdrop, instead I have rough beauty of the Australian bush on one side, the ocean sparkling and deep on the other, and the clear blue sky above. Sitting in contented silence in the carriage, staring out at the Australian landscape, I let go of the stresses of work, ignore the presence of other passengers around me, and be utterly absorbed by my reading, and my notes. So much so that I often came close to missing my stop.

This travel time became the perfect place to capture my thoughts on the knowledge and teachings I was discovering. It has been, I want to stress, an entirely natural and spontaneous process. From the moment I picked up those second-hand books, I have never searched for a particular text, knowledge, or doctrine. Rather, I allowed the path to guide me.

Almost 25,000 words of this book edition is written between 3.30am to 5.30am, and without an alarm my body and mind woke up. Mornings between 3.30 to 5.30 is considered as sacred time and is highly auspicious for spiritual practices, meditation, and self-reflection. People, who have been into a spiritual process, go through a very slow and gradual process of enlightenment. Their development gets manifested in several ways through their bodies, minds, and temperaments. One such very distinct manifestation is when a person starts waking up between 3am to 5am. It is an indication of self-transformation and perfect time to receive the ultimate knowledge. Sun is a vital force that regulates life on our planet. Every moment on earth is defined by its alignment with the sun. The saints and yogis of ancient India studied impact of this alignment and assigned specific tasks to be done at a specific time of the day to get the best out of it. This morning time between 3:30 am to 5.30 am, is defined to be the best time to connect with the higher frequencies of the universe. The phenomenal change takes place during this time. This is the time of possibility which means that the seed of spirituality than has been sown inside you starts sprouting. I am not an early bird but since my time in India, taking care for my father till his death, I became an early bird. Since then, I started waking up early mornings which sets the pace for my day and helps me to focus on the higher goals of life. This is the time; I felt a natural flow of energy and the outcome is this book. A deep feeling of universe guiding me with each word, each chapter and a divine journey.

The writings I have collected and annotated in *The True Self* is where that path has led me. I believe that everything we need to answer the questions that drive us – who am I? What is my purpose? What meaning is there to my life? – has been answered and explored by our ancestors. When reading their words and gathering my notes, I felt energy beyond my body guiding me, freeing me from the feeling of being 'one' to becoming 'whole'. I wish I had come across this knowledge earlier and used my energies with greater purpose. I know that I am not alone in this.

Modern technology means that life, right now, is easier and more convenient than at any other time in human history. For many of us, not only are all our basic needs met, but the world itself is at our doorstep and fingertips. And yet, we are in the grip of a mental health crisis. Tossed by the winds of anxiety, frustration and worry, humanity struggles to find contentment in our relationships, fulfilment at work, and to understand our very identity. Our purpose.

The chaos we see in society today reflects this chaos within us. If we wish to heal society, we need to heal ourselves. Our society and the people within it operate on a worldview that is based on separation. From childhood, we are taught that the world is divided into sides, into likes and dislikes, into good and bad, into self and other. This influences the way we see the world. But separation is an illusion. The Sahara and the Amazon appear to us so distant, so different, that they might as well inhabit separate worlds. And yet they are connected: every year, millions of tons of nutrient-rich Saharan dust cross the Atlantic Ocean, bringing vital phosphorus and other fertilizers to depleted Amazon soils. So, it is with humanity. We are far more connected to everything in the cosmos than we could possibly imagine. And there is hope in that connection.

The solution for the ills that plague humanity is self-transformation. Self-transformation can be achieved not by morals, ethics, attitudinal or behavioural changes, but by experiencing the limitless nature of Who We Are. Self-transformation means nothing of the old self remains. It is a dimensional shift in the way we perceive and experience life. Because life is more than a list of favourite TV shows – or movies, or sports teams, or even people – shared on social media. Its meaning is even deeper than our children, our family, our friends or our career; it is beyond everything we think of as 'real'.

I am fortunate in where I am today, but I have had my share of loss and hardship. My intent in writing *The True Self* is to share the knowledge I have gathered and that has helped me, so it might help others change their thinking and come to a truer understanding. This book is my commentary, rather than a work of original thought. It is my vision, my understanding, the consolidated notes I have drawn up over the years, as I tried to answer the most fundamental questions of life:

Who am I? Why am I here? What is my True Self? What is consciousness? What is awareness? What is the meaning of existence? What is life?

The True Self is a timeless journey that begins 3000 to 5000 years ago, with ancient teachings like Vedas and Upanishads, then moves from Greek philosophers to gurus and saints, yogis, and modern philosophy. It is divided into five chapters, each exploring the teachings and knowledge of various authors and experts: I also shared the content of my podcast, *Conscious Living - Experience the joy within you* in each chapter. Important areas and topics include

Strong beliefs - Faith and religion are good, they give a sense of purpose to our lives and guide us to make the right choices. Interpretation of our own faith and beliefs and how it leads to the truth verses our own truth.

Relationships - Relationships have become main purpose of life, meaningful relationships give us happiness, belonging and sense of purpose to our existence. But relationships have become a point of stress, anxiety and expectations.

Burn the ego - The perfection we seek and look in life is nothing but Ego. The cause of our misery is not outside us, but it is within us as the ego. But how to tell the difference between our True self and our everyday self and understanding our Ego mind.

Separation an illusion - Our society and people within operate on a world view that is based on separation. The universal law of oneness is that we live in a world where everything is connected to everything else.

Inequality why we are biased - Today, wherever people live, they don't have to look far to confront inequalities. Inequality in its various forms is an issue that will define our time. If poverty, injustice, discrimination and gross inequality persist in our world, none of us can truly attain peace and experience life as fair.

Finding clarity in life - If we take 100 individuals who start at the age of 25, they are eager towards life and believe they are going to be successful. But by the time they are 65 years old, only one will be rich, four will be financially independent and others will still be working and or depending on others for basic life necessities. WHY so many fail in life and how to find clarity to fulfill our dreams we had at our young age.

Head versus Heart - Our human mind is manufacturing million ways to suffer. We are confused whether to listen to the head or the heart. This is an ongoing battle within, we all go through in our lives. Understanding how our Mind and Heart works is the key to following Heart rather than Mind. The longest journey we will ever make in our life is from our Head to the Heart.

Food and Energy - Spirituality means Spirit and Matter. Food represents matter and energy is our spirit. Body is an accumulation of food, Mind is an accumulation of thoughts and ideas, but our spirit is our energy. Every individual has within themselves the power to change their circumstances, no matter what they may be by channelling the energies.

Power of Acceptance - Acceptance is a choice but a hard choice in life. We all face challenges in our lives, sometimes they are big ones, sometimes they are small ones, but we all will struggle with them at some point in life. The power of acceptance and self-compassion leads to happiness, pleasantness and peace.

In Silence we speak - In this digital age of constant connection, silence has become a precious commodity. Why being busy has become a badge of honour for everyone and why it is overrated. We are missing out on appreciating the most beautiful and precious moments of our lives.

Happiness a mirage in modern world - Chasing happiness is like going after a mirage, the more we seek it, the further away it gets. Society often makes us to believe and chase different kinds of mirage in the name of happiness.

Peace and pleasantness a ripple effect - All our worry comes from fear, disappointment, or anything we deem as not being the way we want it to be. When we are faced with an obstacle in front of us, we have the ability to put a stake in the ground, make a decision and move forward. We can attain the peace and pleasantness by surrender.

PREFACE

Chapter One: Separation, Inequality, and the Drive to Search for Truth

Ancient knowledge and teachings that were shared over and around 2000 years ago.

The *Vedas & Upanishads* are a collection of Indian philosophical texts that date back to the 8th Century BC. The *Yoga Sutras of Patanjali* date back to India in the 2nd Century BC. *Greek Philosophy* from the 7th and 6th Century BC. *The Tao Te Ching* by Chinese philosopher and writer Lao Tzu (601 - 531 BC)

Chapter Two: Finding Clarity, and the Strength to Follow your Heart

A reflection on knowledge and teachings by authors from around 100 years ago. *The Prophet* by Lebanese American writer Kahlil Gibran (1883 - 1931)

Siddhartha by German Swiss Author Hermann Hesse (1877 - 1962)

Book of Mirdad by Lebanese Author Mikhail Naimy (1889 - 1988)

As a Man Thinketh by British writer James Allen (1864 - 1912)

The Strangest Secret by American radio speaker Earl Nightingale (1921 - 1989)

Chapter Three: From Separation to Union

A reflection on knowledge and teachings by authors since 2015. *Lagom* by Swedish Author Lola Akinmade Akerstrom. *The book of Hygge* by Danish English Author Louisa Thomsen Brits. *Ikigai* by Japanese writer Kenichiro 'Ken' Mogi. *The Yogi Code* by Yogi Cameron Alborzian. *Inner Engineering: A Yogi's Guide to Joy* by Indian Author Sadhguru Jaggi Vasudev

Chapter Four: Acceptance, Silence and Inner Peace

A deep dive into understanding the True Self. <u>Be As You Are</u> and <u>Who Am I: The teachings of Sri Ramana Maharsh</u>i by Indian sage Ramana Maharshi (1879 - 1950)

Chapter Five: Witnessing

A witness to both life and death. <u>International travel during the pandemic</u> to take care of my father till his last breath & finding peace in chaos (2020 – 2021). <u>Clarity over confusion</u> in life explained with ancient wisdom and moral stories.

This is the knowledge that helped me differentiate between my Self, my Mind, and my Body, and liberated me from day-to-day pain and suffering. In all human affairs, there are efforts and there are results, and the strength of the effort is measured by the result. The calmness of mind is the result of a long and patient effort in self-control. A calm person has learned how to govern themselves, and the more tranquil that person becomes, the greater their positive influence on the world. My reading and my notetaking have helped me to control my mind, rather than allow it to control me. The anxiety, stress and frustration of the outside world are no longer reflected in my life. With an inclusive, universal perspective, I can find the pleasantness in life, no matter what it might throw at me.

As I rewrite this preface for this edition, most of humanity has gone through struggles of the coronavirus pandemic. So many of the assumptions we made about our lives have been challenged, so many of the things we thought were so important have been taken away. We were shut out of our temples, churches, mosques, and synagogues. Pubs, sports clubs, theatres, and restaurants are banned. With the change, it has become paramount to stay connected with oneself and contribute towards family, friends, and the vulnerable people in our community. The pandemic has forced us to find a different perspective on the value of life. For many people, it may be the first time they think about life's true meaning. We all experienced a wide range of thoughts, feelings, and reactions around that time, including stress, anxiety, fear, anger, sadness, frustration, disconnection, restlessness and helplessness.

Post pandemic, the humanity especially the western world is struggling with crisis of identity, hashtag activism, divisive politics, gender issues, mental health, sexuality, corporate wokeism, social media misinformation and disinformation. This book is a reflection on what is truly valuable in our lives, and how best to navigate and contribute to the world around us with empathy.

The True Self provides a path for honest seekers of the truth. Approach it openly, and it will guide you, a way to understand and take control of your life. I hope you will see this as an opportunity to open your mind, to discover new directions from ancient wisdom, and most of all, to enjoy reading and finding your own True Self.

Truth is one; Paths are many.

My personal story and connection to the book cover, Mount Fuji and the lake in Japan. *Mount Fuji* is located on the Japanese island of Honshu, with a summit elevation of 3,776.24 m (12,389 ft 3 in). The mountain is located about 100 km southwest of Tokyo and is visible from the Japanese capital on clear days. Mount Fuji is one of Japan's "Three Holy Mountains" along with Mount Tate and Mount Haku. It was added to the World Heritage List as a Cultural Site on June 22, 2013. According to UNESCO, Mount Fuji has "inspired artists and poets and been the object of pilgrimage for centuries". UNESCO recognizes 25 sites of cultural interest within the Mount Fuji locality. The Fuji Five Lake region lies at the northern base of Mount Fuji about 1000 meters above sea level around the lakes Kawaguchiko, Saiko, Yamanakako, Shojiko and Motosuko.

I have never been to Japan, but this image of the book cover came up many times in my meditations and in moments of silence. I am sitting in lotus posture on the land under the maple tree across the lake facing towards the Mt Fuji, and while I close my eyes, an energy within me reaches the summit of the mountain. That energy of the self from the summit, looks at my physical worldly self, sitting in lotus posture across the lake Kawaguchiko, and invites to join my higher self. This experience is very personal and divine for me, as I see my higher self, inviting my day-to-day self to merge and join the ultimate consciousness. This image reflects my higher self, which is peace and pleasantness. A deep connection and the journey of my life and the book.

CHAPTER ONE

Separation, Inequality, and the Drive to Search for Truth

Ancient knowledge and teachings shared over and around 2000 years ago

In 1999, when I was in my early twenties, I went missing. I had just completed a bachelor's degree, and returned to my father's house after years away, at boarding school and then college. It was the first time I had lived with my family since I was eight years old.

My father was excited to have me home, and along with my uncles – who I didn't know well – had my future all mapped out. Not only had they decided that I would become a doctor, like my father/them, but they had also decided whom I should marry. The fact that none of this appealed to me was irrelevant. It was my future, but my opinion didn't matter. Every day his expectation grew, together with my resentment towards him. We argued, we shouted, but none of it made any difference. I wasn't being heard. I wanted to disappear.

One night, when the invisible rope around my neck could not get any tighter, I sneaked out of the house. I stole my father's prescription book, forged his signature, took it to three separate pharmacies and came away with sixty sleeping pills. Then I boarded a train.

The idea of falling asleep and disappearing into the darkness of my mind was more alluring than breathing. Nothing else made sense. I was gone for ten days. Even now, my memory of that time is hazy and incomplete.

I know that I took ten pills before getting on the train, and another twenty while on board. Somewhere along the line, I got off at a train stop, but I don't know where. We must have crossed at least two state borders by this point because the language on the signs had changed. I remember darkness, closed shops, empty streets. I stumbled across a lone vendor selling fruit, chips, and drinks from a four-wheel cart on the train platform. I purchased a *Mango Frooti* – a famous Indian mango-flavoured drink – took the rest of the pills, and laid down on a bench on the platform. I did not expect to wake up again.

Somehow, I got back on the train. I don't know how. I ended up at Surat, a city more than 1300 km away from Tenali, where I started. I vaguely remember being fed by two elderly ladies dressed in white, and then coming to my senses at my friend's house.

He showed me a copy of a local paper, where my parents had placed an ad with my photo and capital letters which spelt MISSING PERSON. When I look back at this episode, there are so many missing details, but that poster, those bold letters, all remain clear.

My friend arranged the travel back to my parents' house, where I was treated to purge the rest of the residue sleeping pills from my system. They also sent me to visit Varanasi for the first time, and while I remember little of that trip, I believe it marked an important step in my journey of self-discovery. I'm sure I caused my parents a lot of pain, especially given the extra pressures of Indian society. Once I returned home, nothing changed. To my family, my actions were just the result of teenage drama, and their answer was to concentrate on my studies and settle down.

Looking back, I'm not proud of what I did. My emotions got the better of me, and I ran away from life rather than dealing with it. But I don't regret it. That sad episode is a part of the person I've become. It is a part of me, but it's not the whole of me. Just like my emotions are a part of me, not the whole me. The difference between myself back then and now is that I understand that concept. Reading ancient knowledge has helped me reach that understanding.

But what led me to this low point in my life? How did I get there in the first place? I was eight years old when my parents sent me to pre-boarding school, and then boarding school, and I completed the rest of my education far from home. From year class six to class twelve, I lived at a boarding school in Korukonda, South India, 750 km away from my parents. The school stands on 206 majestic acres of playgrounds, mango trees, and the Korukonda palace. Many traditional tribal communities live in this area, and while others looked down on them because of their low social standing, I was fascinated by their lifestyle.

The main tribes are the Jatapus, Konda Dora, Savara and the Gadaba. The Jatapus live primarily in the forest and hills and construct traditional homes of wood and mud walls. The Konda Dora build thatched houses on the plains, relying on agriculture and fishing to survive. The Savara community live on the slopes, near streams; the Gadabas in huts on the plains.

Each tribe has their own dialect, other than Telugu – my mother tongue and the most widely spoken language in the state. Often, I would see them selling produce on the side of the road, or within the boundaries of my boarding school. When I stopped to buy fresh mangos or sugarcane, I was struck by the innocence of their lives, and how deeply they were connected to the natural world. Their pure smiles and genuine nature stay with me, fresh in my heart.

During my boarding school days, I only visited my parents once a year, for the summer holidays. Back then there were no smartphones or technology to stay in regular contact. Not only did this give me the freedom to think independently of my family, but it also meant that during my important teenage years, but I had also limited interaction with the broader Indian society.

There has always been a part of me that never felt connected to normal life in South India, to its society or its standards. I was deeply uneasy about the inequality I saw around me: between rich and poor, between genders, based on skin colour or caste. At home, I was not allowed to help my mother in the kitchen because I was the eldest son. If I expressed a desire to help the less fortunate, I was told that god was punishing them for their sins, and instructed to do nothing. As simple a thing as visiting a tea shop in my village was, in my view, plagued by prejudice, and injustice. Lower caste customers were seated on the floor and served tea in glass cups, which they then had to wash. Members of the upper caste drunk tea at a bench, from steel mugs.

Other incidents which left a mark on me, and still play in my head and my heart, are reports I read in the national English newspaper when I was in my pre-teens. In rural India, a low caste man was held in captivity, tortured, and forced to consume human faeces and urine, all because he had an affair with a high caste girl. Low caste girls, on the other hand, were either forced to walk naked in front of other villagers or sexually abused for not following high caste rules. Incidents like these are quite common and have only recently started appearing in Western media.

Separation and inequality still exist, in the name of caste, culture, and religion. Even as a teenager, I wanted to understand *why*. When I dared ask the question, I was told 'it's god's will', or 'it's because they did evil in a previous life'. But driven by my curiosity and already beginning to think independently, I simply could not accept these vague answers, and so began a quest for understanding. A journey towards the truth.

In my teenage years, I invested a lot of time trying to understand religion. I studied Hinduism, Christianity, Islam, Buddhism and Jainism. The more I read, the more I learned, the more I started to realise that all religions are simply different paths towards a single truth. Not only did I read as many texts as I could get my hands on, but I was lucky to connect to others who helped me on my way. One, in particular, a man I met in a tuition class after I finished boarding school, was the first person who was happy to discuss my concerns about Indian society. Skinny, with a rugged beard, he did his best to answer the questions my family and community couldn't or wouldn't. He told me to be careful with my pure soul and protect myself from the unjust world. At the time, I didn't know what he meant, but I followed his advice to examine multiple religions to understand life and the nature of our existence. He taught me not to place limits on my pursuit of knowledge, and to always celebrate the beauty of life. I only knew this man for six months, and he had no idea how much of a positive impact he had on my life. He died within a year after I met him, at a tragically young age, due to illness.

The boy I was at that boarding school, the teenager who questioned the society around him, and especially the lost young man making a desperate train journey, did not have the clarity of mind to understand the life he was living and the actions he was taking. The wisdom I have collected in this book is what gave me the clarity to grow from that boy, that teenager, that young man, to who I am today. It helped me understand the difference between my Self, my mind, and my body. It also helped me understand the world and the society around me.

I moved from South India to Australia just before the 2000 Sydney Olympics. Ostensibly, I did so to further my higher education, but by this point, even my family were forced to admit that I simply did not fit into Indian Society. This way, I could do more than just survive. I could thrive. And I did. The move to Sydney allowed my independence to flourish, and for the first time, I could apply it to every activity in my life, from finding my first job, earning my first dollar, to my relationships and living arrangements. That first job was at a car wash in Sydney – and it was also my introduction to daylight savings. I was told to start at sunrise and finish at sunset and thought that must mean 8 a.m. to 5 p.m. Of course, I didn't realise the sun sets around 8 p.m. in summer!

To understand human beliefs and therefore human behaviour, we should start by examining the two distinct systems of thought that began with our ancestors and are now ingrained as part of our cultures: Eastern and Western philosophy.

Western philosophy focuses on the intellectual mind and the physical body, with an emphasis on ethics and individual behaviour. Eastern philosophy is more spiritual, seeing beyond the mind and body, championing a selfless approach to life and satisfaction with what one has. West aims to analyse and understand the world through objective reasoning, logical deduction and evidence-based observation. While the East rely more on intuitive and spiritual insights to understand and comprehend life's mysteries. Both traditions provide valuable frameworks for understanding of life's most crucial aspects. By exploring both perspectives, we can gain great insights into our own beliefs and find balance between our mind body and spirit.

Western philosophy roots in ancient Greece with notable figures like Socrates, Plato and Aristotle with rich tradition through intellectual debates, various schools of thought, exploring topics like ethics, metaphysics, logic, existence of God, meaning of life, nature of reality and through reasoning challenging our beliefs.

Eastern philosophy took a holistic approach of cause and effect, interconnectedness of all things and pursuit of harmony balance in one life to another.

To put it simply: Western philosophy believes in individualism and Eastern philosophy in collectivism. It should be noted that these days we see a leaning in Eastern society towards the Western lifestyle and ways of thinking, while the Western world trends towards Eastern philosophy.

According to Vadim Kotelnikov (inventor, author, and coach), the main principles of the Eastern and Western philosophies are,

East – Life is a journey towards eternal realities and cosmic unity; A circular view of the universe; The inner world is more important than the physical world; Liberation from the Self is the ideal goal. West – Life is a service; Individualism and the importance of Oneself; The outer, physical world is preeminent; Self-dedication to a goal is ideal; Everything is accounted for within this lifetime.

Broadly speaking: Western society strives to find and prove the truth, while Eastern society accepts the truth as given and is more interested in finding balance. My personal spirit is a combination of the two, travelling across Eastern and Western ideologies, but not limited to either. Both emphasize the importance of developing one's character as a way of achieving fulfilment in life, gain insights into the ultimate reality and our inner selves.

In pursuit of truth, I realised there is your truth, my truth and the truth. So, what is the difference between the truth versus our own truth. They are two different aspects, the truth is simply what it is, and no one can change, manipulate, or alter the truth. But when it comes to our own truth, it is made up based on our own beliefs, faith, culture, and society expectations.

Strong beliefs are the underlying factor for making up our own truth instead of seeing the truth the way it is. Based on the geography, society, community, culture we are born into, our beliefs and behaviours are highly influenced. Since childhood we are conditioned by our parents, schooling, and community standards.

When I reflect on my own childhood, I have experienced how my parents, family, society, and the cinema influenced and conditioned to what I believe. I have been to temples, churches, mosques, cathedrals and did many traditional practices in the name of religion & culture. Majority of the time, I was just following society expectations, family beliefs and practices not knowing WHY am I doing all this. Only in my adulthood, I started to question WHY and challenged these strong beliefs. Don't get me wrong, Faith and religion is good, it gives sense of purpose to our life, and guides us to make right choices in life. Also gives us a path to identify what is right and wrong to lead a meaningful life.

Religion & cinema continues to play a big role with significant geographical variations. In the name of God and truth we continue to create chaos to the humanity instead of harmony and peace. No religion is the new religion which leads to another strong belief.

According to many surveys, Over 80% of the world's population identifies with a religious group. Members of this demographic are generally younger and produce more children than those who have no religious affiliation, so the world is getting more religious. The remaining who has no religious affiliation have strong sense of spirituality or belief in higher force or supreme god or universal spirit, but they don't identify with or practise an organised religion.

So majority of us believe either in god or universal spirit, which leads to the scriptures adopted as their sacred texts. Sacred texts are taken as word of god and considered as the truth. Not knowing what happens afterlife also leads to different strong beliefs. We are all fascinated with miracles, spiritual experiences, divine healings and the supernatural phenomena. Majority of us believe in eternal life if we follow faith, religion or spirituality.

How we interpret our own faith & beliefs is where it leads to the truth versus our own truth. Life can be so harsh at times as to make the truth almost unbearable. So we often try to escape from the truth rather than facing the grim reality. We gain strength when we stop and stare truth in the face. We can experience this in silence. Silence is ever speaking, silence is never-ending speech, silence is the true teaching, suited only for the most advanced seeker. Others require words to explain the truth, but the truth is beyond words. It doesn't admit of explanation. Our duty is to be and not to be this or that. 'I Am that I Am' sums up the whole truth.

I want to share my experience of seeing the truth versus making my own truth when I visited Varanasi. I have been to Varanasi three times, The oldest living city in the world and India's spiritual heart, Varanasi lies on the banks of the Ganges, whose sacred waters flow down from the Himalayas. This city gives an experience of the circle of life and death at one place. City of life and death, nothing out of the ordinary for locals. It is simply the truth in-front of your eyes, it is what it is. Kids playing, monkeys hanging around, sadhus meditating, people dipping in river ganges around the smoke, fire, ringing bells & prayers. In the streets of Varanasi, sandalwood smoke churns through humid air, kicking up piles of red powder left behind from prayers. Humming chants of holy men and the sound of their bells toll alongside the ghats in a rhythmic yet erratic fashion, providing the soundtrack for this spiritual place. For the open-minded and curious, it is one of the most incredible cultural and spiritual experiences.

My first trip, in 1999, was to help me recover from being a lost soul. While I don't remember anything from that time, apart from taking a dip in the Ganges, I know that I was a lost soul. I was vulnerable and lost faith in life when I was a teenager and in my early twenties. I was so confused with everything, trying to understand the truth versus society expectations. When I reflect now, I am glad I was lost, because the journey I have taken completely changed my perspective about life and how I perceive the truth versus the mask I need to wear when performing on the stage of portraying my false self.

My second trip, in 2015, was in response to a calling. All the events in my life to this point – the loss of my mother to cancer, the process of IVF, the breakup of my relationship with my ex-partner and separation from my daughter, being scammed by business partners into near-bankruptcy – ignited a longing within me to return. But more than that, I felt called to Varanasi, and the truth as well. The trip itself was effortless, with none of the difficulties that usually arise when travelling from South

India to North India at the peak of winter. The energy I felt in this trip is close to enlightenment, discovering my true self and understanding purpose of my existence. All my life struggles seem nothing and pointless compared to life itself. I understood in this trip, the truth is always there, and it takes for the individual to see it as it is without a mask.

My third trip, in 2019, exactly twenty years from my first visit, felt like a witnessing. Every aspect of that journey I witnessed in peace, because I felt I had reached the Source like the river reaching the ocean. The Source is understanding my True Self & finding the truth. It is consciousness and a constant state of pleasantness. The Source is within one's own Self – the rest is seeking. The Source is in our heart, where we all meet as one and don't judge. Seeing the truth the way it is without making any judgments or amendments. To practice this in day-to-day life can be very challenging as it doesn't meet the society expectations.

I know this recent trip to Varanasi will not be my last. I still see it every day, images and memories rising to the quiet surface of my mind. Within me, there is a deep call to return. I look forward to what that next trip will bring.

People in search of *moksha* (meaning liberation) have been travelling to this northern Indian city for centuries. Liberation is nothing but seeing the truth versus living in our own truth. To reach the heaven we must die first, similarly, to see the truth we have to destroy the ego which is our own truth based on our own beliefs. This place is not pretty, clean or beautiful, just like the saying by Lao Tzu - *The truth is not always beautiful, nor beautiful words the truth.* This place made me to experience the truth which is not always beautiful. The truth is as it is and can't be altered, changed or tampered. Perceptions and perspectives can change our opinions, but they can never alter the truth. The truth remains unwavering regardless of the change of seasons and manipulation by our minds.

The Vedas and Upanishads

And so, we begin with the Vedas and Upanishads. The Vedas and Upanishads are the oldest written texts on the planet and date back to the beginning of Indian civilisation. They are not strictly speaking religious texts, but rather focus on seeking ways to perceive and understand life.

The Vedas are rituals strongly rooted in Indian culture and Hinduism, connected with everyday practices, such as drawing in chalk on the front doorstep for auspicious fortune, offering food to the gods, and so on. The Vedas are primarily concerned with rituals, rites, religious customs, traditions, and applications. The Upanishads are primarily concerned with spiritual enlightenment.

I am more interested in the Upanishads. They are the most important part of the Vedas and focus on the purpose of life, its higher meaning, the nature of existence and ways of understanding the universe. The Upanishads have helped me grow in my understanding of existence, the circle of life, the meaning of god, and the different states of mind and spirit within ourselves, by explaining many aspects of life from a universal viewpoint. They are not limited to religion, geography, or people.

Vedas means Knowledge: The Vedas are perhaps the oldest written text that exists on our planet as they date back to the beginning of Indian civilisation. They are supposed to have passed through oral tradition for over 50,000 years and came in written form between 4000 to 6000 years ago.

Vedas reflect the practical wisdom resulting from the reflection of life as it is. Vedic devotion and belief stand on the practical wisdom of cosmic and human reality, and it is not limited to religion. Part of Vedas I came across Samskara meaning rite of passage to understand the full life cycle from conception, birth to death. A ceremony or event making an important stage in someone's life, especially birth, the transition from childhood to adulthood, marriage and death. Samskara is a Sanskrit word, derived from two roots, sam meaning well planned or well thought out, and kara meaning the action undertaken. It is believed that actions performed with full awareness have the greatest impact, leaving impressions for better life. A beautiful way to appreciate, celebrate and understand all stages of life.

In this modern-day mundane life where lot of things are taken for granted, the samskaras can be the ancient antidote to appreciate life. There are 16 samskaras beginning from right before the birth of a child to even after the death to keep enriching human life. If you are feeling unhappy about life or lacking purpose and meaning towards life, it is time to visit these 16 stages of life to feel gratitude, joy and happiness in life. The relevance of these relevance of these samskaras is to celebrate and share the significant chapters of your life with your loved ones, garner their best blessings, make prayers together to strengthen positivity, and take a break from the chaos of daily life.

There are 4 samskaras before the birth of a newborn, 11 samskaras during their life, and 1 samskara after the soul leaves the body.

Conception is the first samskara begins before the birth of a child. It requires modern-day parents to nurture positive thoughts and great health to conceive a healthy, beautiful, and intelligent child. It is a private rite of passage, marking the pure intent of a couple to have a child.

Prayers for fetus protection the second samskara is performed during the third or fourth month of pregnancy. The ceremony celebrates the rite of passage of developing fetus, marking the stage where the baby begins to kick as a milestone in a baby's development. The father of the child prepares a special dish for his wife to celebrate the good health of both the child and the mother. Depending on the culture and personal preferences, prayer is performed for the well-being of the child by family members.

Parting hair and baby shower the third is performed during the 7th month of pregnancy, this samskara celebrates motherhood and encourages positive emotions in the soon-to-be mother. It involves the inclusion of close family members and friends who make the mother feel special with gifts and blessing the child in her womb. The husband parts wife hair three times to assure unconditional love and support. As the last three months of pregnancy are very hard, this ritual frees her from her worries and gives her time to relax and enjoy.

Birth ceremony the fourth is post-natal samskara performed on the 6th day of the child's birth is rite of a newborn infant. The ritual acts as a great way to share your happiness of becoming a parent with your family and friends. It also requires the father to touch the lips of the baby with honey for a beautiful father-child bonding moment.

Ceremony of naming a child the fifth plays a significant role throughout an individual's life. For this reason, a name is given to the newborn after great consideration while considering the position of the moon during the baby's birth and its sun sign. This rite of passage is usually done on the 11th or 12th day after the birth. It is believed a good name will determine your child's success and good fortune.

Child's first outing the sixth works as another major bonding ritual between the child and its parents. Going out and coming forth is the rite of passage where the parents take the baby outside the home and the baby formally meets the world for the first time. The parents also introduce child to the five elements, earth, water, fire, air, and ether. It's a great way for the couple to spend some quality time with their child by showing the sun at sunrise or sunset and or the moon.

Child's first solid food the seventh is celebrated with great cheer and happiness when the child is fed with solid food for the first time. Feeding of food is the rite of passage marks the first time a baby eats solid food, typically containing cooked rice mixed with honey. Ceremony is performed in the 6th month of the child's birth or shows first teeth, family members and friends come together to worship the goddess of food and grant blessings for the child's good health. Some parents include charity and feeding the poor to mark this milestone.

Child's first haircut the eighth marks the introduction of personal hygiene and cleanliness to the child. The rite of passage marks the child's first haircut typically the shaving of the head. The ceremony plays a major role in one's life and is celebrated with grandeur. Sacred texts are chanted, and prayers are made for the fast development of the child's intellect. This ceremony is seen as a passage of purity.

Beginning of education, the ninth is child's first day at school deserves to be remembered and celebrated. On this day, the parents take some time to pray to the Goddess of Knowledge along with their child. This develops deep respect in the child's heart for knowledge and art. Beginning of study is the child's formal attempt to learn means of knowledge.

Piercing of the ear the tenth is the piercing of a child's ear celebrated. The purpose of this optional ritual is primarily an ornamentation of the body, and it is part of the baby's socialisation process and culture emersion. The piercing is usually done with a clean gold thread, or silver needle. For a baby boy, the right earlobe is pierced first and for a baby girl, the left earlobe. In case of girls, the left nostril may also be pierced. The significance is the child, he or she grows up, of beauty and social presence.

Child's going to school the eleventh is the rite of passage symbolises the leading or drawing towards the self of a child, in a school by a teacher. It is a ceremony in which a guru or teacher accepts and draws a child towards knowledge and initiates the second birth that is the young mind and spirit. The child was also given a sacred thread to wear a symbol of entering formal education. In modern times, this ritual can still be celebrated in its modified form regardless of age to teach the children the role of discipline and moral values to get ahead in life.

Study of sacred ancient scriptures the twelfth is the rite of passage that marked the start of learning the sacred ancient scriptures. In ancient India, the student's preparation involved helping with school chores, living a simple life, going to villages to seek donations of food, collect wood and bring water, cooking and general maintenance of school by sharing with school community and teachers. The child learns responsibility and other important aspects of life's wisdom through ancient moral values and intelligence.

Celebrating the onset of Puberty the thirteenth is first shave of youth's facial hair, beard or moustache typically around 16 years old. The coming-of-age ceremony ended with student reciting his vow of chastity till marriage. For girls, it is observed wearing clothes (changing from children's clothes to teenage clothes to accommodate the body changes) and receiving gifts from family and friends, which signifies the crossing the stage of puberty. Our ancestors, celebrated puberty and menstruation as an important stage of life and there was no stigma.

Graduation the fourteenth is the ceremony associated with the end of formal education and vows of chastity. Typically, significant time lapse happens between end of education and marriage as the ceremony occurred after completion of 12 years of school, that would be reaching around 21 years of age.

Marriage the fifteenth is the rite of passage and rituals associated with marriage. Undoubtedly, marriage is the most important phase of anyone's life. It is celebrated depending on the different cultures around the world. The wedding rites and ceremonies begin with engagement of a couple and extend to rites of passage after the completion of wedding. With family and friends around sacred rites, prayers, blessings, the couple enter a blissful phase of lifelong commitment and happy memories. The act of first sexual intercourse happens after the wedding.

The Last rites the sixteenth is the rite of passage performed in harmony with the sacred premise that the microcosm of all living beings reflects a macrocosm of the universe. The soul or spirit is the essence an immortal that is released at the ritual. The last rite of passage returns the body to the five elements air, water, fire, earth, space and its origins. The last rites are usually starts within a day of death and then go on for the next 13 days, which include rituals and prayers for safe passage of the soul.

Every culture, religion and faith celebrate these stages of life in their own traditional way. This is a reminder; life is a beautiful gift that deserves to be celebrated and treasured as we pass each milestone. Our actions performed in one lifetime will be passed on to future generations, so these are associated with the theory of karma. Our actions shape the moral and spiritual development of an individual and are the root of both pleasurable and painful interpretations of life experiences.

Our ancestors and ancient wisdom already gave us all the answers we are seeking about life, and Upanishads is one area our ancestors passed on through generations.

Upanishads are parts of Vedas and the content is philosophical in nature. The Upanishads are commonly referred to as Vedanta, meaning the last chapters of the Vedas and alternatively as objects the highest purpose of the Veda. Upanishads speaks about the supreme or the highest knowledge. The concepts of ultimate reality, soul and self are central ideas in all the Upanishads.

The origin of Vedic and Upanishads concept is dated back to the Indus valley, by the people of Harappan civilisation around 7000 BC. Their concepts were then exported to Central Asia during Indo-Aryan migration. Central Asia people referred to themselves as Aryans meaning noble or free and having nothing to do with race, merged their beliefs and culture between India and Persia. Indo-Aryans the modern-day India and Iran are part of a larger nomadic group and with their nomadic lifestyle, the knowledge has been passed on to as far as Europe.

Modern era historians have discussed the similarities between the fundamental concepts in the Upanishads and major western philosophers. The spread of the Upanishads to the west happened in the 17th-century. Sanskrit, the written language of Upanishads, was truly a foreign language for most scholars in Europe and Upanishads were practically unknown. Persian translation of the Upanishads first exposed them to the west. Then a Frenchman translated Persian into Latin which got the interest and attention of Europeans in ancient Indian cultures.

Greece is often considered the cradle of western civilisation. When we hear the word philosophy, most of us relate to Greek philosophy due to widely known Greek philosophers. Modern philosophy as we know of it in the modern era, owes its creation to India and Greece. Many seekers of the truth in the past came across the knowledge of Upanishads, this includes Persians who translated Upanishads from Sanskrit language to Persian language, through them became accessible to the major parts of Europe. Greek culture has influenced western civilisation, we must not forget that ancient Greeks themselves were influenced by the knowledge from Indian saints and philosophers.

It is believed that after the arrival of Alexander the Great in 326BC, the gates of India opened for Greek influence. The Greek historian and geographer Herodotus in 5th century BC describes the land as India calling it *he Indike Chore* meaning the Indus land. The Greek colonies in Asia Minor the western and central Turkey were already part of the Achaemenid empire since 546 BC. Thus, the Greeks and Indians encountered each other as subjects of the empire. The direction of Knowledge started to flow from east to west. Pythagoras theory of mathematics was already known in India. In the writings of Plato and Aristotle, you will see the influence of Upanishads especially the theory of illusion and immortality of the soul. The Upanishads also influenced Plato's predecessor and mentor Socrates. If we look into the Stoic philosophy which believed in a cosmos formed and guided by a reason, order, destiny, and the law of nature. The origins of stoic ideas go back beyond the Greek philosophers to the philosophies of the East. According to many European philosophers, the texts of Upanishads are the production of the highest human wisdom, beneficial to understand life and death, deeper meaning of know thyself by knowing the difference between the ego self and the eternal self to peaks of consciousness. The conception of wisdom that came to the Greeks from these sources was one of pursuing inner peace, seeking finally the state of nothingness that alone frees a human being from the pain and struggle of existence.

Upanishads have inspired many in the west to think radically differently from what they have been taught. Unlike the Vedas which present the rituals relevant to a specific culture, the Upanishads teachings attempt to be universal.

Four main Vedas are Rigveda is knowledge through Praise & Hymns; Yajurveda is knowledge through Worship & Prose; Samaveda is knowledge through Songs & Melody; Atharvaveda is storage of knowledge.

Each Veda is sub-classified into four parts Samhitas consists of prayers, mantras & benedictions; Aranyakas is about rituals, ceremonies and observances; Brahmanas is commentaries on the rituals, ceremonies & sacrifices; Upanishads is philosophical dialogues on meditation, philosophy & spiritual knowledge.

Vedas present a unified vision of the eternal order revealed by the universe and how one is supposed to live in it. We can see similar knowledge in other teachings.

Kalpa Sutra - The text in Kalpa Sutra holds great honour by the sect of Jainism, a religion of India. It deals with the lives of 24 Jains saviours, pontiffs, monks recording the descent from heaven, birth, initiation, obtaining of omniscience and death. The date Kalpa Sutra was composed was estimated about 2,300 years ago.

Analects - The Analects are a collection of the teachings and thoughts of Confucianism. The philosophy of the Analects is marked by an absence of metaphysical speculation and concern above all for the correct social and political ordering of human society. Confucian philosophy is not based upon transcendent principles or upon a reward and punishment based upon what happens after death. Instead, Confucius argued that social reform cannot come from above and without but rather from within, from within the human heart.

Tao Te Chung - Taoism is an outlook on the fundamental nature of life and the universe. The word Tao is nothing less than an expression of the profound unity of the universe and of the path human beings must take to join, rather than disturb that unity. The path begins with an understanding of the origin of the universe, knowing the ancient beginning is the essence of the way.

Tripitaka - The earliest collection of Buddhist scriptures. The texts of Tripitaka are organised into three major sections - First Discipline on the rules of the communal life of monks and nuns, Second Disclosure teachings on doctrine & behaviour focusing on mediation techniques from Buddhist senior disciples, Third Higher knowledge interpretations and analyses of Buddhist concepts.

Upanishads means sitting down near (Upa - Near, Shad - To sit); Out of 200 surviving Upanishads, the below 13 are considered most important.

Isa teaches the importance of seeing the self in every creature and the unity of the individual soul with the ultimate reality, advocating for a life of action in the world without attachment as unity of the self and the world.

Kena rejects the concept of intellectual pursuit of spiritual truth claiming one can understand only through self-knowledge.

Katha emphasises the importance of living in the present without worrying about the past or future.

Prasna is to understand the existential nature of the human condition.

Mundaka explains the difference between spiritual knowledge to intellectual knowledge and why spiritual knowledge is more important for self-realisation.

Mandukya deals with the spiritual significance of the sacred syllable of OM to peace from life's distractions and stress.

Taittiriya addresses that duality is an illusion and the impact on one's happiness.

Aitareya emphasises the human condition and joys in life lived in accordance with good morals and values.

Chandogya states that all self's are interconnected and one. The inmost essence of all beings is same, the whole world is one truth, one reality, one self.

Brihadaranyaka deals with higher self, the immortality of the soul, the illusion of duality and the essential unity of all reality.

Svetasvatara discusses the relationship between the self and higher self and importance of self-discipline as means to self-realisation.

Kausitaki focuses on the unity of existence and illusion of individuality which causes people feel separated from one another.

Maitri focusses on nature of self and liberation from suffering through self-realisation.

The vedic sages tried to explain the purpose of life and meaning to our existence through Upanishads. Human beings have five senses and use them to live a life of survival, but the sages asked, what was it that is enabling an individual to sight, smell, hear, taste, touch, move, find food, feel emotions and procreate. The sages came up with an answer that everyone has a higher self within the self. This higher self is divine and not limited by our five senses.

Our purpose and existence of life is to connect and reunite with our higher self, the source we come from. This realisation leads us to duality as an illusion. There is no separation between individuals, as everyone has this same divine essence within them, and everyone is on the same path, in the same universe, towards the same destination. One is already what one wants to become; one only must realise it. The goal of life, then, is self-realisation to become completely aware of and in touch with one's higher self, so one can live with the eternal order of universe and after death return home to complete union with higher self or pure consciousness.

Everyone was thought to have been placed on earth for a specific purpose which was their duty which need to perform with the right action (Karma) to achieve self-actualisation or self-realisation. The concept of karma is that one's actions always have consequences, the individual's management of his or her own actions will lead one to either success or failure and satisfaction or sorrow. If a person failed to perform their duty in one life, their past actions would require them to return to try again, another opportunity to live and lead a conscious life. This cycle of rebirth and death is known as samsara and one can find liberation from samsara through self- realisation. When a person achieves Moksha (Liberation), their Atman (Self) returns to the source. Like a drop of water returning to the ocean. Some rivers flow to the east, others to the west, they become one with the sea, they become the sea and just as these rivers, when they are in the sea, do not know, I am this river or that; in the same manner, we return to the source without any duality.

Upanishads are not created to provide answers but to provoke questions for an individual to find their true self and meaning of life. I have taken below notes as a summary to understand Upanishads for my own self.

The Lord or God means the soul of all and the inmost Self - The absolute Reality. Everything in the universe, all things one sees, feels, thinks, or imagines are under the god. The god is none other than our indwelling Self. The only reality or truth is one Self and the world is one divine self.

Spirit is known through revelation. It leads to freedom, it leads to power. Revelation is the conquest of death. The living person who finds spirit finds the truth. The person who can see the same spirit in every creature cling neither to this nor that, attains immortal life.

There is a chariot which has five horses pulling it, the horses have reins in their mouths, which are in the hands of a charioteer, a passenger is sitting at the back of the chariot.

> The body is the chariot itself.
> The five senses (Indriya) are chariot horses.
> The reins in the mouth of horses are the mind (Manas).
> The intellect (Buddhi) is chariot driver.
> The objects, desires, pleasurable things perceived by the senses is the chariots path.
> The self (Atman) is chariots passenger (Higher Self).

In the material world, the mind doesn't exercise restraint on senses (horses), so the intellect (Charioteer) submits to the pull of the reins (mind), leading to a path of pleasures and desires that the soul (passenger) is not satisfied. However, if the passenger wakes up to the higher nature and purpose to lead the charioteer in proper direction, the driver can then govern the mind and senses towards a meaning direction. Till then we feel life is meaningless and with no fulfilment or contentment.

All things fly to the self, as birds fly to the tree for rest.

OM is the conditioned & unconditioned spirit. The wise person with its help alone can attain the one or the other.

> Meditate on Syllable A alone a person is soon born again on this earth.
> Meditate on 2 Syllable A & U a person goes to the moon & after enjoying its pleasure, return to earth again & again.
> Meditate on 3 Syllable A, U & M is joined to the light of the sun. Meditate AUM indicates the supreme reality.

If you meditate on 3 syllables in separation, it is the emblem of mortality, but if you meditate all together, inseparable, interdependent, the 3 conditions physical, mental, intellectual reward the individual & goes beyond mortality. The three states of consciousness are waking state, dreaming state and deep sleep.

> A (Outward) is the state of wakefulness
> U (Inward) is the dream state
> M is the deep sleep with no desire

The one who sees the dream is the mind. During the dreamless deep sleep, this mind merges into supreme reality. It is the final refuge of elements, then self feels bliss & harmonious.

The root cause of the universe is spirituality which is spirit & matter, food represent matter & from food semen is produced & from semen life is born. Life originates from the soul, life force comes to the body by the soul's will & divides to 5 forms.

> Apana an elimination of waste by lungs & kidney etc
> Vyana an expansion & contraction of muscles
> Udana is the sound and vocal
> Samana is digestion & metabolism
> Prana is the heartbeat & breathing

Every society and individual are influenced by religion directly or indirectly. Truth is one but seers express it in many ways. God is one but expressed in many ways through knowledge of self-realisation. It is the soul that reveals to the seeker Its true nature.

> Mind comes from food, life comes from water, speech comes from light.
> Speech is above name, Mind is above speech, Will is above mind.
> Meditation is above substance; Wisdom is above meditation.
> Power is above Wisdom; Food is above power.
> Water is above food; Light is above water.
> Air is above light; Memory is above the air.
> Hope is above memory; Life is above hope.

Life lives by life, life gives life, life gives for life, life gives power. Life is father, mother, sister, brother, tutor & guide. Life is all. If an individual feels & knows this, the reason is deeper than discussion. A person who knows the truth goes beyond discussion.

Self is the bridge, when you cross that bridge, you shall see, if sick, you shall be well, if unhappy, you shall be happy. Heaven is those that are masters of themselves. They can move anywhere in this world at their pleasure.

When a person is fast asleep, at peace with himself, happy, without a dream, then that is self. That is the unalarmed, immortal spirit.

An old legend from ancient scriptures says. there was a time when human beings & gods were equal. But we misused our divinity for power, greed and privilege. Seeing this, the Creator decided to take the divinity away from humans and hide it somewhere they could never find.

The question raised by gods, "Where could divinity be hidden so that humans would never find it?" All the gods had a meeting to decide where to hide divinity.

"Let's bury it deep in the earth," said one god. But the other answered, "Humans will dig into the earth and find it."

"Why not sink it in the deepest ocean bed, they could never find their divinity there" suggested another god. But the others thought, "That won't do, humans will learn to dive into any ocean and will find it."

Another suggested, "Let's hide it on the top of the highest mountain." everyone replied, "Human beings will eventually climb every mountain to take back their divinity."

There seemed no place on earth or sky that humans wouldn't reach. After deep thought process, they found a solution where to hide human divinity.

We will hide their divinity deep into the centre of their own being. Humans will hunt for it on the highest mountain, in the deepest sea, in the densest forest and on the toughest road, but they will never seek their divinity inside themselves.

Everyone was very happy and agreed that there couldn't be a more perfect hiding place for the most precious gift of God. Ever since, we humans have been searching relentlessly all over the earth for something that already lies within ourselves. We have explored every mountain, sea, temple, church, mosque, river, tree and bird on earth. We even seek our divinity in the sun, the planets and the stars, but we never looked inside of ourselves.

The Divine is omnipresent and ever-present, but the only place to connect with the Divine is the core of our own being.

Patanjali

Patanjali is believed to be an author and first teacher of yoga. Patanjali gives insights into how the energies within us can be maintained for better thinking and actions. Raja Yoga, an eight-step process to personal transformation, gives a better understanding of our mind and body. It enables us to differentiate between selfish and selfless thoughts, which are linked to our experience of pain and pleasure. For my own personal growth, I started by identifying the following four stages, which are present in every situation in life:

First is the view of my world and my point of view. Second is to view with empathy and another person's point of view. Third is the ability to view without an emotional reaction. Fourth is to understand things in a holistic or universal way

Patanjali was a sage who lived at least 1700 years ago, everything you hear and experience about yoga came from him. No one knows much about his birth or his life. But anonymity is typical of the great sages of ancient India as they recognised the outcome as a group effort. And while in western society is fashionable to practice yoga, I wonder how many heard about Patanjali.

Patanjali is a treasure to be read and referred to again and again by seekers. His teachings on ethics, meditation, physical postures provide directions for dealing with situations in daily life.

The following quotes from different passages of the book 'The yoga sutras of Patanjali' by Swami Satchidananda. Our goal in life is to keep the serenity of our minds. Human beings fall into four categories or locks, sukha means happy people, dukha means unhappy people, punya means the virtuous and apunya means not so virtuous. Patanjali gives four keys to these locks, which are maitri means friendliness and kindness, karuna means compassion, mudita is delight and upeksha is disregards and equanimity.

Use the friendliness key when you see a happy person, being able to share in another person's happiness or good fortune, instead of being jealous or trying to take away their joy through jealousy.

Use the compassion key when you see an unhappy person, being able to help or comfort a person who is upset or struggling, instead of taking pleasure in seeing someone else suffer.

Use the delight key when you see a virtuous person, feel delighted and appreciate the virtuous qualities instead of feeling envious.

Use the disregard key when you see a not so virtuous or wicked person, being able to develop calmness and equanimity towards those whose actions oppose our values, instead of judging and wasting our energy.

According to the book, there are 196 Sutras (holy text) traditionally divided into four chapters or sections. These texts discuss the aims and practice of yoga towards liberation, enlightenment, freedom, peace and pleasantness. The main essence of yoga is the progressive settling of the mind into silence. When the mind is settled or still, we are established in our own essential state, which is pure consciousness, peace and pleasantness. Your true self lies hidden in the silence between your thoughts and beyond all limitations. Our essential nature is often clouded by the activity of the mind.

Contemplation (samadhi) - Gives theory of yoga and description of the most advanced stages of the practice of Samadhi (super conscious state). The art of yoga by understanding our mind activity, movements of consciousness by practice and detachment.

Practice - Philosophy more of physical nature. It outlines in a practical way how to attain freedom and a new life. The practice of the first five steps of Raja Yoga which are abstinence, observance, posture, breath control & withdrawal of senses.

Accomplishments - The final three steps of raja yoga, concentration, meditation & contemplation are powers accomplishments which could come to the faithful practitioner. All the accomplishments come as by-products of your yoga practice.

Absoluteness - Yoga from a more cosmic and philosophical viewpoint. It's an experience of absoluteness, unlimitedness, and infinity.

Patanjali's Raja Yoga offers an 8 steps approach for personal transformation. Being aware of these eight steps and practising regularly could bring clarity in life, reduce anxiety and stress.

Yama is correct behaviour towards others. Abstinence, moral principles and self-control by non-accumulation of possessions, non-violence, truthfulness, not stealing, and not wasting life energy.

Niyama is the principles by which you should live your own life. Observance, ethical principles by purity, contentment, self-control, self-discipline, study of spiritual scriptures, and pure devotion to self.

Asana is the postures to prepare the body to be a fountain of consciousness. Posture practice by control of our bodies and physical exercises.

Pranayama is expanding the life force through breathing exercise. Breathing control through connection between breath and emotion.

Pratyahara is turning the senses inward to explore the inner world, sense withdrawal. Introspection and withdrawal of the senses from external objects.

Dharana an effortless focussed attention and training the mind to meditate. Concentration to focus one's thoughts and feelings.

Dhyana a continuous flow of consciousness, a state of meditation perfected. Meditation happens when the mind is quiet, no imagination.

Samadhi is a union with the body, the mind, the breath, the soul, a state of blissful presence. Super conscious state and complete realisation. Samadhi is where the knower, knowledge and object of knowledge unite.

If we can observe our mind in slow motion, we will be able to understand our thought process and the consequences of our actions. For example take mind in action - Mind consists of Buddhi (Intellect); Manas (Memory); Chitta (Awareness); Ahankara is I (Identity).

While you are sitting in solitude in peace, a nice smell from the kitchen. Manas (Memory) records getting a nice smell. Buddhi (Intellect) discriminates what is that smell? I (Identity) think it is cheese. How nice, what kind. Swiss; Swiss cheese and Buddhi decides 'yes, I should have some now'. All three happens one at a time, but so quickly that we seldom distinguish between them. Until you have the cheese, your mind won't go back to its original peaceful condition.

The Want is created, then the effort to fulfil the Want, and once you fulfil it, you are back to your original peaceful position. So normally before want is created, you are in a peaceful state, that is the natural condition of the Mind.

All the differences in the outside world are the outcome of your mental modifications (the thought forms, workings of the mind). The entire outside world is based on your thoughts and mental attitude. The entire world is your own perception.

SEPARATION, INEQUALITY, AND THE DRIVE TO SEARCH FOR TRUTH

As the mind, so the person. Bondage or liberation are in your own mind. If you feel bound, you are bound. If you feel liberated, you are liberated. There is nothing wrong with the world, you can make it a heaven or a hell based on your approach.

You (Self) abides in its own nature. You are that true seer. You are not the body nor the mind. You are the knower or seer. You always see your mind and body acting in front of you. You know that the mind creates thoughts, it distinguishes and desires. The seer knows that but is not involved in it.

The true you are always the same, but you appear to be distorted or mixed up with the mind. Making the mind clean and pure, you go back to your original state. The pure 'I' without attached identity is all same energy whether animate or inanimate. Behind different forms of energy there is one unchanging consciousness or spirit or self. However, as we start to grow that one spiritual heart becomes self-conscious, and like the trunk of a tree splits from one truck into many branches of ego, mind, intellect rise to fluctuations, afflictions, separation and differences of ourselves. Through practice, we begin to discriminate between the trunk, the branches, shoots, flowers, fruits and bring everything back to its single pure state which is our true self.

Selfish thoughts bring pain and pleasure, while selfless thoughts bring neither pain nor pleasure. Every desire binds you and brings restlessness. To get liberation you have to be completely desireless. As long as the mind is there, its duty is to desire. The secret is that any desire without any personal or selfish motive will never bind you.

The truth of self is always the same, but when presented through words, forms and modes it may appear in different ways to suit the individual or age etc. the sources of right knowledge are direct perception, inference and scriptural testimony.

If you accept the existence of a finite space, automatically you accept an infinite space. The thought of one implies the thought of the other. So we feel our mind and knowledge are limited and finite, so there must be a source of infinite knowledge beyond. When you transcend the mind through proper concentration, you feel the cosmic force. Only in silence can you / you will be able to understand the higher soul or being.

In one sense you are the witness, in another, you are the actor. It depends on where you put yourself. In reality, you are the witness, but if you miss reality, you are the actor. When you become the actor, you are responsible for your actions, when you are the witness, you are not responsible for your actions, because you are not acting. So, either act and be responsible or allow the mind and body to act and be a witness totally free from bondage and attachments.

Analogy of Hand – Understanding the energies is very simple, through hand gestures you will notice great outcomes on concentration and awareness. For example, being in a sitting posture with a straight back, place your palms facing upwards on your legs and notice your breathing. Now your palms downwards and notice where the air is coming in and out. You will notice the difference of breathing from the diaphragm when downwards and from the heart when palms upwards. This is a simple but effective way to say how powerful our energies work within us by our postures.

According to Shaivism one of the ancient traditions within Hinduism the five-syllable mantra Na Ma Shi Va Ya represents the five elements, five senses and five fingers. This mantra purifies our actions by connecting the self to the universal oneness of five elements

NA - Earth (Ring Finger) represents the first chakra related to survival issues on an emotional level, the right to belong and to have. It is found at the base of the spine between the anus and genitals. *MA* - Water (Small Finger) represents the second chakra related to issues around sexuality on an emotional level, the right to feel and to desire. It is located a little below the navel. *SHI* - Fire (Thumb) represents the third chakra related to emotional issues centre around themes of personal power, the right to act and stand in one's power. It is located above the navel and below the sternum. *VA* - Air (Index Finger) represents the fourth chakra related beyond the lower three densities of the animal soul and allows an opening to love, the right to love and be loved. It is located at the heart centre. *YA* - Space (Middle Finger) represents the fifth chakra related to space dealing issues around expression, the right to speak and be heard. It is located at the throat centre.

Different postures of hand while meditating has their own meaning to improve your health and energy levels. The use of hand gestures during meditation carries specific goals of channelling your body's energy flow.

The Laws of the Universe

Even as a teenager, I was fascinated by the laws of the universe. This fascination started the day I realised that everything is connected: I am part of the universe, and the universe is a part of me. During my childhood and summer holidays, I visited many temples with my family. Temples are part and parcel of Indian culture and lifestyle. The most famous temples in India run in a straight line, from north to south at 79° E 41'54" longitude.

India, which was called Bharat in ancient times, included modern-day Afghanistan, Pakistan, India, Sri Lanka, Bangladesh, Burma, Malaysia, Nepal, Vietnam & other Asian nations. The ancient Maharishis, Sadhus and Rishi Munis of Bharat – the 'saffron-clad half-naked ascetics', as they were 'fondly' called by the West – were great scientists. Their temples were built according to the Vedic sciences and are thousands of years old. The 79° E 41'54" longitude line was the centre of India in ancient times and held great importance. As per the ancient Vedic calculations of Vaastu (architecture), important Temples were consciously built on this vertical axis to strengthen and radiate universal energies, making it possible to utilise these energies in an efficient way.

As an example, the five most famous temples to Lord Shiva located in the south of India represent the five elements of air, water, earth, fire, and space:

The temple for water is in Thiruvanaikaval, the temple for fire is in Thiruvanamalai, the temple for air is in Kalahasthi, the temple for earth is in Kanchipuram and the temple for space is in Chidambaram

To think that our ancestors deciphered that this geographical line was the vertical centre of India, without modern-day technology like satellites or GPS, is truly inspiring. Every year, my family and I visited Tirupati Temple, one of the temples in this longitude line, and my father's birthplace. In doing so, I learned about the science, knowledge, and education systems of the ancient Indian peoples, and I was enthralled by how advanced they were. Much more than we like to imagine today.

The universal laws made even more sense as I began to apply them to my daily life, my activities, and how I responded to the situations I was presented with.

In my thoughts and actions, I practice the twelve most important laws of the universe. I even keep them, as well as the world population clock (www.worldometers.info), on my phone as a reminder not to limit my perception, and to curtail my own Ego. Some examples of these laws are:

The law of oneness says we live in a world where everything is connected. The law of cause and effect helps me rely on thoughts before emotions. The law of energy says that everyone has within them the power to change the conditions of their lives. Sadly, only a small percentage of humanity ever utilises this power. From the law of gender, we learn about masculine and feminine energies. These energies are not based on physicality, but we all carry both. Because of the way we are raised in our societies, most individuals are never able to balance these energies

A few popular television shows have helped my understanding too, such as Brian Cox's *Forces of Nature* and *Life of a Universe*, and Neil DeGrasse Tyson's *Cosmos: A Space Time Odyssey*. These documentaries explain the universe in simple ways, making wisdom accessible to anyone curious about our existence. The beautiful storytelling by the hosts, their pure passion about our universe and nature, deeply resonated with me.

To me, the laws of the universe are a balance between science and philosophy, and I believe they constitute ancient knowledge, so I have included them in this book. They are embedded into every culture and teaching, whether Hinduism, Islam, Christianity, Buddhism or other knowledge. The Kybalion (which is the teachings of the Kabbalah) focuses on seven hermetic principles to explain the nature of self and our existence. The hermetic principles can be traced back to ancient Egypt and Greece, serving as tools for the priests and pharaohs of Egypt, the philosophers of Greece, then the artists and inventors of the Italian Renaissance, and modern revolutionaries and leaders. Knowingly or unknowingly, our ancestors used these laws to understand the universe and the reason for our existence.

The universe runs on natural laws and when we take time to understand them, we can leverage them to live better lives.

The laws of universe - 12 laws of the universe we can apply to our daily lives. Everything is energy and that's all there is to it. Match the frequency of the reality you want, and you cannot help but get that reality. It can be no other way. This is not philosophy this is physics. The quote said by Albert Einstein. The 12 laws of the universe are the governing principles of everything that happens within us and in the universe.

This is a listening universe and it's always listening to every thought, feeling and word you ever uttered; even when you didn't know about the laws. You have been manifesting everything that you have in your life today through these laws, whether or not you knew about them.

These laws are what have been the basis of everything from the tiniest atom to the largest star or sun. These laws give way to what is already in our minds. It is believed that the one who understands each of these laws to their fullest is the one to hold the key to the master of this universe. Some of our ancient philosophers and thinkers believed and implemented these laws in their lives. This is why they were perpetually content and grateful for everything they ever promised received because they were manifesting everything into their lives with their mere thoughts. Your thoughts are not just powerful, they are the key to your life.

Law of Divine Oneness - We live in a world where everything is connected to everything else. Everything we do, say, think and believe affects others and the universe around us. Energy is everything all at once and it flows through everything living or inanimate. We will see our own reflection in the people and things around us. It means that the better we think about others, the better it comes back to us and become us.

Law of Vibration - Everything in the universe moves, vibrates and travels in circular patterns. The same in the physical world apply to our thoughts, feelings, desires and wills in the Etheridge world. Each sound, thing and even thought has its own vibrational frequency, unique unto itself. What you are feeling in the current moment determines your vibration and subsequently the frequency you are on.

Law of Action - Action must be applied for us to manifest things on earth. Therefore, we must engage in actions that support our thoughts, dreams, emotions and words. The law further states that you must do the things and perform the actions necessary to achieve what you are setting out to do. Unless you take actions that are in harmony with your thoughts and dreams and proceed in an orderly fashion towards what you want to accomplish there will be no foreseeable results. Thinking about something and talking about it is different from following through with it. Action set into motion our thoughts and desires.

Law of Correspondence - The principles or laws of physics that explain the physical world (Energy, Light, Vibration &

Motion) have their corresponding principles in the etheric or universe. Whatever you are thinking or feeling within is exactly what is happening outside your mind and body, and this relates to every object, place or person you encounter. The reason why sometimes most of what we want never manifests is because we are constantly lying and in denial about our most raw and genuine thoughts and feelings. This corresponds with everything from our health, jobs, money and relationships.

Law of Cause & Effect - Nothing happens by chance or outside the universal laws. Every action has a reaction or consequence, and we reap what we have sown. Every thought, action or word by you is a cause and every reaction, feeling or assumption that is created through that cause is an effect. What's goes around comes around.

Law of Compensation - The law of cause & effect is applied to blessings & abundance that are provided for us. The visible effects of our deeds are given to us in gifts, money, friendships, inheritance and blessings. Each person is compensated in like manner for that which he or she has contributed. One shall always be compensated for the efforts and contribution, whatever it may be however much or however little. So, if you invest only for today, you will benefit only for tomorrow. If you invest for a lifetime, you will never stop reaping the benefits. If the law of cause and effect ensures that each of your thoughts and actions returns to you, the law of compensation ensures the quantity and quality of those returns.

Law of Attraction - Demonstrates how we create the things, events and people that come into our lives. Our own thoughts, feelings, words and actions produce energies which in turn attract the energies. Negative energies attract negative energy, positive energies attract positive energy.

Law of Energy - Everyone has within them the power to change the conditions in their lives. Higher vibrations consume and transform lower ones, thus each of us can change the energies in our lives by understanding the universal laws and applying the principles in such a way as to effect change. Every individual has within themselves the power to change their circumstances, no matter what they may be. Simply put the energy from the formless realm is constantly flowing into the material world and taking form. This energy is limitless and inexhaustible. The energy in the universe is constantly moving from one object or individual into the other.

Law of Relativity - Each person will receive a series of problems, life's trials and errors for the purpose of strengthening the light within. Take this as a challenge and remain connected to heart when proceeding to solve the problems. No matter how bad we perceive our situation to be, there is always someone who is in a worse position. It is all relative. Everything in our material world is made real only by relationships or in comparison with other things. True self-esteem and true humility arise out of that realisation in the eyes of the ego, self-esteem and humility are contradictory, in truth they are one and same.

Law of Polarity - Everything is on a continuum and has an opposite. We can suppress and transform undesirable thoughts by concentrating on the opposite pole. It is the law of mental vibrations. Where there is black, there is white; where there is darkness, there is light; where it is good, there is also bad. Henceforth this is why we can change our flow of thoughts or frequencies easily. The law of polarity validates that this is a universe of duality, everything exists in twos.

Law of Rhythm - Everything vibrates and moves to certain rhythms. These rhythms establish seasons, cycles, stages of development and patterns. Each cycle reflects the regularity of the universe. Masters know how to rise above negative parts of a cycle by never getting too excited or allowing negative things to penetrate their consciousness. Everything happens for a reason. Every vibration has a certain rhythm to it and that's how it attracts another vibration that falls into the same pattern or rhythmic flow.

Law of Gender - Everything has its masculine Yang and feminine Yin principles and are the basis for all creation. The spiritual initiate must balance the Yang and Yin energies within herself or himself to become a master. Gender is not limited to physical appearance. This is the law that governs creation and in its simplest understanding states that everything in nature is both male and female. Both are required equally for life to exist. No one is greater or lesser than the other and both sides are inhabited within everyone irrespective of whether or not one is male or female.

Relationships are a good measure of life to experience the laws of universe. Relationships have become main purpose of life, meaningful relationships give us happiness, belonging and sense of purpose to our existence. Making connections with other individuals and maintaining these relationships develop a sense of meaningfulness in life. Doesn't matter what type of relationship, do not burn the boat after crossing the river. I feel like the burnt boat in majority of my relationships. I get burnt to ashes and they leave me with no choice but to keep raising out of ashes like a phoenix.

Whether it is parents, family, friends, my partners and or ex partners, all I heard from them is I am arrogant, strong head, stubborn, manipulative, narcissistic, not committed, challenging, distant & from another planet. Well, I don't blame them for me not playing the society expectations and not meeting their conditional love. I was always seeking unconditional love, whether is it motherly love, fatherly love, siblings love, romantic love, children love or in a marriage regardless of my short comings. I am aware I am not perfect, and I am aware that I have many flaws and vulnerabilities.

I was sent to boarding school at a young age and unfortunately, I did not experience unconditional love, everything turned out to be either conditional or I haven't lived to their expectations. I was eight years old when my parents sent me to pre-boarding school, and then boarding school, and I completed the rest of my education far from home. From year class six to class twelve, I lived at a boarding school in South India, 750 km away from my parents. During my boarding school days, I only visited my parents once a year, for the summer holidays. Back then there were no smart phones or technology to stay in regular contact. Not only did this give me the freedom to think independently of my family, but it also meant that during my important teenage years, I had also limited interaction with the broader community and society.

So, I had no communication with my parents or family, leading to not experiencing motherly love, fatherly love and family love. This made me to be independent and most of times I didn't know how to be in a relationship as I didn't experience or see any role models during my childhood the importance of relationships. I always craved for unconditional love, which is accepting anything the other person does without protest, even if its hurtful to you or them, it doesn't mean doing everything the other person wants you to do and expecting them to do the same. You can't love someone unconditionally unless your love remains unchanged despite their actions. Most people experience unconditional love from their mothers and that relationship is never ending.

My mother died at a young age with cancer, so that motherly love is something I feel deep inside me missing when I think of relationships, and how it impacted on all my other relationships. I want to share a poem from Khalil Gibran about relationships, which can be related to every type of relationship

> You were born together, and together you shall be forever more.
> You shall be together when the white wings of death scatter your days.
> And, you shall be together even in the silent memory of God.
> But let there be spaces in your togetherness,
> And let the winds of the heavens dance between you.

Love one another, but make not a bond of love:
Let it rather be a moving sea between the shores of your souls.
Fill each other's cup but drink not from one cup.
Give one another of your bread but eat not from the same loaf.
Sing and dance together and be joyous, but let each one of you be alone,
Even as the strings of the lute are alone though they tremble with the same music.

Give your hearts, but not into each other's keeping.
For only the hand of Life can contain your hearts.
And stand together yet not too near together:
For the pillars of the temple stand apart,
And the oak tree and the cypress grow not in each other's shadow.

This poem summarizes an unconditional love doesn't matter the type of relationship but experiencing the truth, which is unconditional versus our own truth, which is majority of times conditional. There are many truths in a personal relationship, your truth versus their truth is not the same. If we dig deep enough, we start to see all the conditions.

The beginning of love or relationship is to let the other person be perfectly themselves and not to twist or turn them into what you want them to be. The truth is letting the person being themselves and accepting them with all the vulnerabilities they come with, our own made-up truth is trying to change the person with conditions and creating boundaries. No wonder most people are unhappy with relationships because of not being true to themselves or for not letting others to be true to themselves.

Every relationship has love and that love is the glue which sticks together. But if that love is controlling, conditional then slowly the glue falls off.

Love is a quality, not something to do with somebody else. Every action that we do is in some way to fulfill certain needs.

People have physical, psychological, emotional, financial and social needs to fulfill. Don't fool yourself into believing that the relationships you have made for convenience, comfort and well-being are relationships of love. The moment there is a condition, it just amounts to a transaction. Maybe convenient transaction and arrangement. Love need not necessarily be convenient, most of the time it is not. It takes life, you must invest yourself. A love affair need not be with any person, you could be having a great love affair and relationship with life itself.

We are all imperfect and those who love your imperfections will always love you. A beautiful story I would like to share about imperfections.

The Story of the Cracked Pot, A water bearer had two large pots, each hung on each end of a bamboo stick which he carried across his neck.

One of the pots had a crack in it, and while the other pot was perfect and always delivered a full portion of water at the end of the long walk from the stream to his house, the cracked pot arrived only half full.

For a full year, this went on daily, with the bearer delivering only one and a half pots full of water in his house. Of course, the perfect pot was proud of its accomplishments, perfect to the end for which it was made. But the poor cracked pot was ashamed of its own imperfection and miserable that it was able to accomplish only half of what it had been made to do.

After a year of what it perceived to be a bitter failure, the cracked pot spoke to the water bearer one day by the stream. 'I am ashamed of myself, and I want to apologize to you.'

The bearer asked, 'Why? What are you ashamed of?'

The pot replied, 'For the past year I am able to deliver only half of my load because this crack in my side causes water to leak out all the way back to your house. Because of my flaws, you don't get full value for your efforts.'

The water bearer felt sorry for the old, cracked pot, and in his compassion, he said, 'As we return to my house, I want you to notice the beautiful flowers along the path.'

As they went up the hill, the old, cracked pot took notice of the sun warming the beautiful wildflowers on the side of the path, and this cheered it somewhat. But at the end of the trail, it still felt bad because it had leaked out half its load, and so again it apologized to the bearer for its failure.

The bearer said to the pot, 'Did you notice that there were flowers only on your side of the path, but not on the other pot's side? That's because I have always known about your flaw, and I used it. I planted flower seeds on your side of the path, and every day while we walk back from the stream, you've watered them.

For a year, I have been able to pick these beautiful flowers to give to my wife and daughter and decorate my house.

Without you being just the way you are, i would not have this beauty to grace and give joy to my family.

Flaws and weaknesses are natural parts of life. Better a diamond with a flaw than a pebble without.

Nobody on this earth is perfect.

Ancient Egyptian Afterlife - To reflect and measure on our lives

I was fascinated about Ancient Egyptians efforts made on afterlife journey of the soul. The central cultural value of ancient Egypt was harmony and balance. Which maintained the order of the universe and the lives of the people, similar to the laws of the universe. Keeping balance in one's life encouraged the same in one's family, neighbourhood, community, society and the entire nation. A vital aspect of maintaining this balance was gratitude which would elevate a person's journey through life and, after death, allows one's heart lighter than a feather to the god Osiris in the Hall of Truth before passing on the paradise of the Field of Reeds. On the other hand, Ingratitude was the "gateway sin" which opened the soul up to all the negative energies of doubt, distrust, envy, bitterness, and self-centred absorption. Through prayer, festivals, and personal religious observances, one could maintain a light heart, enjoy a full life after bodily death, and that one would not be judged harshly by Osiris and lose one's hope of paradise.

According to the world history article of The Egyptian Afterlife & The Feather of Truth, Ancient Egyptians believed in afterlife. Ancient Egypt has long been known as a formidable civilization with a unique set of beliefs around the afterlife. The ancient Egyptians believed in a life beyond death, known as the Field of Reeds, where they would be reunited with loved ones, joy, luxury, and gain eternal life. Ancient Egyptians believed that the journey to the afterlife began at death and depended largely on their deeds in life. Thus, they prepared for death by accumulating wealth, passing knowledge to their children, engaging in rituals to ensure passage, and ensuring that their bodies were perfectly preserved and taken care of after death.

Many ancient Egyptians believed that there was a place they went to when they died called the *Duat*, translates to 'underworld' or 'afterlife'. To get to the afterlife, a deceased person's spirit had to travel on a long and challenging journey. Each person was made of essence (*ka*) and personality (*ba*), which joined together in the afterlife to form a perfect being called an *akh*. The *ba* was usually shown as a human-headed bird. The deceased travelled through the underworld in his own form and in the form of the *ba*. The goal was to reach a special place called the Field of Reeds – Egyptian heaven.

Since ancient Egyptians believed that the journey to the afterlife began immediately after death, they were focused on burial ceremonies as well as mummification rituals. Funerary practices were deeply rooted in religion, culture and traditions. In general, the journey for the dead was long, arduous and it included tests, moral dilemmas, and other obstacles. It was believed that the spiritual process of mummification was the key to a successful transition into the afterlife. This meticulous process included removing internal organs, treating the body with natron, bandaging and wrapping the body, opening the mouth, and placing objects such as beads, amulets, and statues inside the coffin. Magical spells and prayers were also recited during the rituals for the dead. It was believed that these rituals and spells would provide the deceased with the necessary protection to guarantee their safe passage into the afterlife, and that these objects would give them strength and courage to traverse the afterlife.

To reach the eternal paradise of the Field of Reeds, however, one had to pass through the trial by Osiris, Lord of the Underworld and The Hall of Two Truths, which involved the weighing of one's heart against the feather of truth.

Ancient Egyptians believed that upon death they would be asked two questions, and their answers would determine whether they could continue their journey in the afterlife.

The first question was, 'Did you bring joy?'

The second was, 'Did you find joy?'

The answers to those two questions determine their passage to Egyptian heaven.

To the ancient Egyptians believed it was not only possible but highly desirable to have a heart that is lighter than a feather. The afterlife of the ancient Egyptians was known as the field of reeds, a land of no sickness, no disappointment and no death. One lived eternally by the streams and beneath the trees which one had loved so well in one's life on earth.

To reach there, one maintained a light heart by embracing gratitude for all one had been given in life and turning aside negative thoughts and energies. Ingratitude was considered a gateway sin that drew one down a dark path toward selfishness and sin. Sins were understood as thoughts and actions contrary to the value of harmony - which the white feather symbolized, that separated one from others as well as from the gods. The worst of these sins was covetousness because it expressed ingratitude for the gifts one had been given and illicit desire for the gifts of another.

Ancient Egyptians warns against covetousness, a strong desire and wish to have something that belongs to someone else, citing its dangers and consequences. If you desire your conduct to be good, to set yourself free from all evil, then beware of covetousness which is an incurable disease. It is impossible to be intimate with it; it makes the good friend bitter, it alienates the trusted employee from his master, it makes bad both the father and the mother, together with the mother's brothers, and it divorces a man's wife...Do not be covetous regarding division when food or goods are dispensed between you and others and do not be exacting with regard to what is due to you. Do not be covetous towards your family. Covetousness made the soul heavy with sin because it encouraged pettiness, jealousy, self-pity and, especially, expressed ingratitude. These sins made impressions on the soul which weighed down the soul's "heart" and made it impossible for one to pass through the Hall of Truth and find paradise. This was a major concern for the ancient Egyptians who understood that their life on earth was only one part of a much longer journey.

A person's soul was thought to be immortal, an eternal being whose stay on earth was only one part of a much larger and grander journey. This soul was said to consist of nine separate parts:

Khat was the physical body
Ka was one's double-form
Ba a human-headed bird aspect which could speed between earth and heaven
Shuyet was the shadow self
Akh the immortal, transformed self
Sahu and *Sechem* aspects of the *Akh*
Ab was the heart, the source of good and evil
Ren was one's secret name.

All nine of these aspects were part of one's earthly existence and, at death, the *Akh* (with the *Sahu* and *Sechem*) appeared before Osiris in the Hall of Truth and in the presence of the Forty-Two judges to have one's heart (*Ab*) weighed in the balance on a golden scale against the white feather of truth.

The ancient Egyptians recognized that when the soul first awoke in the afterlife it would be disoriented and might not remember its life on earth, its death, or what it was to do next. In order to help the soul continue on its journey, artists and scribes would create paintings and text related to one's life on the walls of one's tomb, now known as the Pyramid Texts, which then developed into the coffin texts and the book of the dead.

The *Pyramid Texts* are the oldest religious works from ancient Egypt dated to c. 2400-2300 BCE. The *Coffin Texts* developed later from the *Pyramid Texts* in c. 2134-2040 BCE while the *Egyptian book of the dead* was created c. 1550-1070 BCE. All three of these works served the same purpose: to remind the soul of its life on earth, comfort its distress and disorientation, and direct it on how to proceed through the afterlife. Along with these directions, prayers were inscribed on the walls of tombs asking Osiris (and other gods) to show mercy to the soul.

In the *Egyptian Book of the Dead* it is recorded that, after death, the soul would be met by the god Anubis who would lead it from its final resting place to the Hall of Truth. Images depict a queue of souls standing in the hall and one would join this line to await judgment. While waiting, one would be attended to by goddesses such as Qebhet, daughter of Anubis, the personification of cool, refreshing water. Qebhet would be joined by others such as Nephthys and Serket in comforting the souls and providing for them.

When it came one's turn, Anubis would lead the soul to stand before Osiris and the scribe of the gods, Thoth in front of the golden scales. The goddess Ma'at, personification of the cultural value of harmony and balance would also be present, and these would be surrounded by the Forty-Two Judges who would consult with these gods on one's eternal fate.

The soul would then recite the Negative Confessions in which one needed to be able to claim, honestly, that one had not committed certain sins. These confessions meaning that the soul strove in life to devote itself to matters of lasting importance rather than the trivial matters of everyday life. Each sin listed was thought to have disrupted one's harmony and balance while one lived and separated the person from their purpose on earth as ordained by the gods. In claiming purity of the soul, one was asserting that one's heart was not weighed down with sin. It was not the soul's claim to purity which would win over Osiris, however, but instead, the weight of the soul's heart.

The 'heart' of the soul was handed over to Osiris who placed it on a great golden scale balanced against the white feather of Ma'at, the feather of truth on the other side. If the soul's heart was lighter than the feather then the gods conferred with the Forty-Two Judges and, if they agreed that the soul was justified, the person could pass on toward the bliss of the Field of Reeds.

According to some ancient texts, the soul would then embark on another journey through the afterlife to reach paradise and they would need a copy of the Egyptian Book of the Dead to guide them and assist them with spells to recite if they ran into trouble. According to others, however, after justification it was only a short journey from the Hall of Truth to paradise

The soul would leave the hall of judgment, be rowed across Lily Lake, and enter the eternal paradise of the Field of Reeds in which one received back everything taken by death. For the soul with the heart lighter than a feather, those who had died earlier were waiting along with one's home, one's Favorite objects and books, even one's long-lost pets.

Should the heart prove heavier, however, it was thrown to the floor of the Hall of Truth where it was devoured by Amenti (also known as Amut), a god with the face of a crocodile, the front of a leopard and the back of a rhinoceros, known as "the gobbler". Once Amenti devoured the person's heart, the individual soul then ceased to exist. There was no 'hell' for the ancient Egyptians; their 'fate worse than death' was non-existence.

It is a popular misconception that the ancient Egyptians were obsessed with death when, in reality, they were in love with life and so, naturally, wished it to continue on after bodily death. The Egyptians enjoyed singing, dancing, boating, hunting, fishing and family gatherings just as people enjoy them today.

The elaborate funerary rites, mummification, and the placement of Shabti dolls were not meant as tributes to the finality of life but to its continuance and the hope that the soul would win admittance to the Field of Reeds when the time came to stand before the scales of Osiris. The funerary rites and mummification preserved the body so the soul would have a vessel to emerge from after death and return to in the future if it chose to visit earth.

One's tomb, and statuary depicting the deceased, served as an eternal home for the same reason - so the soul could return to earth to visit - and shabti dolls were placed in a tomb to do one's work in the afterlife so that one could relax whenever one wished. When the funeral was over, and all the prayers had been said for the safe travel of the departed, survivors could return to their homes consoled by the thought that their loved one was justified and would find joy in paradise. Even so, not all the prayers nor all the hopes nor the most elaborate rites could help that soul whose heart was heavier than the white feather of truth.

Life in the Field of Reeds reflected the real world they had just left with blue skies, rivers and boats for travel, gods and goddesses to worship and fields and crops that needed to be ploughed and harvested. The dead were granted a plot of land in the Field of Reeds and were expected to maintain it, either by performing the labour themselves or getting their shabtis to work for them. *Shabtis* (small statuettes) were often supplied with agricultural tools such as baskets and hoes and were often led by a foreman or overseer.

The Field of Reeds was the second life where the dead regained new life. It was a paradise created to match the place of their highest desires. The souls would spend eternity in the Field of Reeds, rejuvenated as youth with access to food, love, and joy. The Field of Reeds was the Kingdom of the gods, and it was believed to be a place of abundance and wealth. It was a physical manifestation of the ultimate reward for a good life – eternal bliss.

The ancient Egyptians believed that the deceased were reunited with their families in the Field of Reeds, where they could spend their days in contentment and peace. The afterlife was described as an everlasting state, and the Field of Reeds was said to provide eternally prosperous and happy lives. Those who lived in the afterlife were forever rid of worries, sadness, and toil, and could explore the beauty of nature and the world with peace and joy.

This Egyptian afterlife is not just a story, but a way of living life with morals. Those who lived a life with morals and values will be rewarded. We can apply this ancient wisdom into our modern life, to find some barometer of morality and good versus bad.

An atheist was seated next to a farmer on an airplane and turned to him and said, "Do you want to talk? Flight time goes quicker if you strike up a conversation with your fellow passenger." The farmer, who had just started to read his book, replied to the total stranger, "What would you want to talk about?" "Oh, I don't know," said the atheist. "How about why there is no God, or no Heaven or Hell, or no life after death?" as he smiled smugly. "Okay," he said. "Those could be interesting topics but let me ask you a question first. A horse, a cow, and a deer all eat the same stuff – grass. Yet a deer excretes little pellets, while a cow turns out a flat patty, but a horse produces clumps.

Why do you suppose that is?"

The atheist, visibly surprised by the farmer's intelligence, thinks about it and says, "Hmmm, I have no idea." To which the farmer replies, "Do you really feel qualified to discuss God, Heaven and Hell, or life after death, when you don't know anything about shit, ie horse shit, deer crap & cow dung?" The atheist didn't utter a word and the farmer enjoyed reading his book the whole flight time.

In faith, there is enough light for those who want to believe and enough darkness to blind those who don't. Faith is important in life; faith is hope, it gives strength and courage to face the world. Whether you believe in religion or not, faith is something we all have within us, a beacon of light guiding us during the times of turmoil. Beliefs are opinions that you form about from reading, hearing, seeing or learning and they can change over time, where as faith it is different. Faith doesn't have doubts and questions, doesn't require proof or evidence. It simply is like the truth. Belief clings and faith let go. The believer will open his mind to the truth on condition that it fits in with his preconceived ideas, opinions and wishes. Faith on the other hand is an unreserved opening of the mind to the truth, whatever it may turn out to be. Faith has no preconceptions, and it is a plunge into the unknown. It takes courage to have faith and be faithful

Faith shapes our values, relationships, morals, service to others and social responsibility. It takes courage for someone to have a good faith in something without any evidence or proof. In that belief itself we can see the power of faith, power of God, power of universe, power of higher power and power of humanity.

Ancient Greek Philosophy

I was attracted to Greek philosophy in my late twenties, after my move from India to Australia. Seeking answers about life lead me to the teachings of philosophers such as Socrates, Plato, and Aristotle. Greek philosophy is widely known. It forms the basis for much of the philosophies and societies in the West and is also studied in other parts of the world. For this reason, I will not focus too much on it here but will stick to the basics. In my research, I explored the evolution and teachings from both pre- and post-Socrates Greek philosophy. The work that connected to me the most was *Consolations of Philosophy* by Alain de Botton. In this text, he explores unusual aspects of the lives of philosophers including Socrates, Epicurus, and Seneca, such as being unpopular, not having enough money, feelings of frustration, feelings of inadequacy, or living with a broken heart.

The death of Socrates and the death of Seneca both captured my mind and became important moments for me to reflect on. I believe they summarise how a person can be true to themselves, even in the face of death. Both men were forced to commit suicide, with their friends and family beside them.

Socrates was convicted of moral corruption and impiety and sentenced to death by drinking hemlock. His influential friends gave him the choice to go into exile, but he declined. Socrates declared that he was not afraid of death and that it would undermine his life's teachings if he were to run away. So, while all his friends were crying, Socrates took the hemlock and said, 'You are strange fellows, what is wrong with you? I sent my wife away for this very purpose, to stop creating such a scene. I have heard that one should die in silence. So please be quiet and keep control of yourselves.'

Socrates walked until his legs grew heavy, then he lay on his back until the poison reached above his waist. His last words were to his friend, 'Crito, we owe a cock to Asclepius. Do pay it. Don't forget.'

There are a lot of similarities between Seneca and Socrates' death. Seneca was born around 4BC in Cordoba, Spain, was destined for great things from birth. Wealthy and well educated, he was the first to arrive and last to leave from school. The most powerful lesson that Seneca learned was the desire to improve practically in the real world and take away with him one good thing every day. While his commitment to self-improvement was beloved by his teachers, his father was not a great fan of philosophy. Seneca served as leading adviser to emperor Nero but was ordered to commit suicide on suspicion of planning a coup. Seneca followed stoicism, a philosophy that believes finding an inner kingdom of the mind is the way to find happiness in life. At his suburban villa outside of Rome, Seneca opened his veins, took hemlock, and died in a steam bath. He died slowly but fearlessly in the presence of friends and family. He wrote extensively about death in his teachings: 'You live as if you were destined to live forever, no thought of your frailty ever enters your head, of how much time has already gone by you take no heed. You squander time as if you drew from a full and abundant supply, though all the while that day which you bestow on some person or thing is perhaps your last'.

The decisions we make in life and the way we face their end makes these two deaths worth reading and understanding. The world keeps spinning when we're gone and yet so many of us live life arrogantly, as though we are destined to live forever. But as Socrates put it, the unexamined life is not worth living, a life that is not enriched by reflection is no better than death. We can explore our existence beyond our daily chores of work, and family.

Our ability to do philosophy is one of the things that differentiates us from other animals. Philosophy is embedded in everything, and we all have philosophies that form the basis for our motivations and what we do with our lives. But for most of us, those philosophies are unexamined and automatic and instinctual. Western world philosophy can be dated back to with famous Socrates 2,500 years ago. The ancient Greeks believed philosophy was a medicine for the soul. Most of the ideas in contemporary cognitive therapy come directly from Ancient Greek philosophy and it gives us an understanding of emotions, stoicism and habits.

Emotions are connected to our beliefs and opinions. Habit that philosophy must be a daily practice.

Around 304 BC, a merchant named Zeno was shipwrecked on a trading voyage. He lost nearly everything and on his way to Athens, he was introduced to philosophy and became the origin of Stoicism. Stoicism says you cannot control what happens to you, you can only control how you react to it. The stoics believed that the practice of virtue is enough to achieve happiness and a well lived life. The path to achieve happiness is spent practicing the four virtues in everyday life, wisdom, courage, moderation and justice. The best indication of an individual's philosophy was not what a person said but how a person behaved. To live a god life, one had to understand the rules of natural order since stoics believed everything was rooted in nature. Stoicism is a tool in the pursuit of self-mastery, perseverance and wisdom to live a good life.

Greek philosophers broke the traditional and sought rational explanations, their speculation also formed the early basis for science and natural philosophy. As Socrates said the strong minds discuss ideas, average minds discuss events, weak minds discuss people. Socrates was a Master of Philosophy, and he never wrote anything and most of his philosophical contributions come through his students, mainly Plato.

The teachings of Socrates focussed on discussion, argument and dialogue to find out the truth. The only good is knowledge and the only evil is ignorance. He believed that people made immorally wrong life choices because of their lack of knowledge and unless they examined their lives and gained wisdom, people would continue to make mistakes in ignorance. To gain wisdom, everyone needs to reject the traditional beliefs, concern for ethical issues and have conversation as a practical method to acquire knowledge. We should get to know ourselves as best as we can as the real insights can come only from within.

Socrates beliefs and realistic approach in philosophy led to his end, as he was tried and convicted for criticising religion and corrupting the youth. He chose death by suicide over exile, his death is a great academic view of philosophy and life itself.

I remember reading this story of Socrates and the three sieves. Sieve is a utensil consisting of a wire or mesh used for straining solids or liquids. One of the acquaintances of the great philosopher Socrates came up to him and said:

"Socrates, do you know what I just heard about one of your students?"

"Hold on a moment," Socrates replied.

"Before you tell me, I would like to perform a simple test. It is called the Three Sieves Test." The man was not familiar with the three sieves, so Socrates continued:

"Before you say a word about my student, take a moment to reflect carefully on what you wish to say by pouring your words through three special sieves."

"The first sieve is the Sieve of Truth. Are you absolutely sure, without any doubt, that what you are about to tell me is true?"

"Well, no, I'm not. Actually, I heard it recently and…"

"Alright," interrupted Socrates. "So, you don't really know whether it is true or not.

Then let us try the second sieve: the Sieve of Goodness. Are you going to tell me something good about my student?"

"Well…no," said his acquaintance. "On the contrary…"

"So, you want to tell me something bad about him," questioned Socrates, "even though you are not certain if it is true or not?"

"You may still pass the test though," said Socrates, "because there is a third sieve:

the Sieve of Usefulness. Is what you want to tell me about my student going to be useful to me?"

"No. Not so much." said the man resignedly.

Finishing the lesson, Socrates said: "Well, then, if what you want to tell me is neither true nor good nor useful, why bother telling me at all?"

When the man bowed his head in shame, Socrates smiled and said "Well, next time you like to share anything with me, please make sure it is either true, good or necessary."

In today's digital age of social media looking for instant gratifications and validations, this story of three sieves can be applied to avoid fakeness & negativity.

According to the philosophy of Plato by Irwin Edman, The Ethics of Socrates may be stated as follows:

Men aim at the good. No man voluntarily chooses evil. To do evil or to choose evil is a matter of lack of insight; the central virtue turns out, therefore, to be knowledge. Health, Wealth, beauty, all these are good in so far as they are well used. And good use of the goods of life demands knowledge of their appropriate employment. If we knew how to convert stones into gold, they would be of no use to us unless we also knew how to use the gold. Knowledge of good and evil, knowledge of that part of one's Self, the soul, which alone can measure, estimate, choose, is the central wisdom, and wisdom is the essential virtue of which all the virtues turn out to be simply special instances or parts.

For the fear of death is indeed the pretence of wisdom, and not real wisdom, being a pretence of knowing the unknown; and no one knows whether death, which men in their fear apprehend to be the greatest evil, may not be the greatest good. It is not this ignorance of a disgraceful sort, the ignorance which is the conceit that a man knows what he does not know.

Plato believed that reality is divided into two parts, the ideal and the phenomena. The ideal is the perfect reality of existence. The phenomena are the physical world that we experience, and it is a flawed echo of the perfect, ideal model that exists outside of space and time. He called this the theory of forms, which asserts that the physical world is not really the real world, instead ultimate reality exists beyond our physical world.

When having a deep conversation, Plato structured to have a meaningful dialogue, by begin with a simple question in which nothing is presumed. The question is then examined, and definitions given. Then the assumptions are questioned. Finally, the conventional views are dismissed or redefined.

Aristotle made important contributions to ethics and happiness. Happiness is the perfection of human nature. Since man is rational animal, human happiness depends on the exercise of his reason. Happiness depends on acquiring a moral character, where one displays the virtues of courage, generosity, justice, friendship in one's life. The concept of Eudaimonia, people achieving happiness through leading lives which combine cultivation of their intellects and moral activity.

Perfect human happiness is to be found in the activity which is proper to human beings, and which fulfils their essential nature. This is not by engaging in philanthropy and doing good works, but by intellectual activity. The intellect is the highest thing in human beings apprehending the highest forms of knowledge, such as philosophical and scientific truths. Leading the life of thought or a contemplative life is how human beings fulfil their purpose. The happiest human beings will be those who think.

Epicurus was the founder of Epicureanism, which is minimalism, moderation and simple pleasures of life. Happiness comes from moderation, simplicity, friendship and community. An approach to life that stresses finding happiness through loving a simple life. The epicurean happiness list of life necessities and link to happiness are

> Natural and Necessary is friends, food, freedom, shelter, clothes, and thought. These are also the main sources of anxiety, death, illness, poverty, superstition.
> Natural but Unnecessary is the grand house, private baths, banquets, servants, overindulgence of meat and fish.
> Neither Natural nor Necessary is the fame, status and power.

When we seek beyond what is natural and necessary, we fall into our own Ego. Epictetus was a Greek stoic philosopher was born as a slave in modern Turkey. He taught that philosophy is a way of life and not simply a theoretical discipline. To Epictetus, all external events are beyond our control, he argues that we should accept whatever happens calmy and dispassionately. However, individuals are responsible for their own actions, which they can examine and control through rigorous self-discipline. Five lessons from Epictetus to improve your life. Wealth consists not in having great possessions but in having few wants. There is one way to happiness and that is to cease worrying about things which are beyond the power of our will. If you want to improve, be content to be thought foolish and stupid with regards to external things. It is impossible for a man to learn what he thinks he already knows. Nature has given men one tongue but two ears, that we may hear from others twice as much as we speak.

If you are really seeking change in life, then you need to dive deep into seeking, knowing and understanding your true nature versus your egoistic self. The perfection we seek and look in life is nothing but our Ego. The cause of your misery is not outside you; it is you as the Ego. The Ego mind is insecure and keeps us in constant misery, by contrast the true self, the truth is who we really are and is connected to the All that is. Our Ego is the main catalyst for our own truth versus the truth. Only when we destroy our Ego we see the Truth. We need to burn our ego before it burns us. In life one of the hardest things to do is to let go of our ego.

Ego mind is the impressions of thoughts and words projected onto us as children from adults that knew no better, ideas from already negative people, beliefs that were pushed onto our pure clean state of being. This ego is what we have learned about ourselves from others, from experiences, and from parents, society, community we grew up in. We have been conditioned since were kids, and it is important to understand that this is not your real You, it is only what you learned to think who you are and there is a whole world of difference between that and your own true self or the truth. The ego mind is arrogant and simply wants to believe what was conditioned to believe rather than seeing the truth as it is.

How to tell the difference between your true self which is the truth and your everyday self which is your own truth.

The purest part of an individual is the true self, in other words it is our spirit or soul. When you experience the moments of love, stableness, peacefulness and pleasantness that is the truth or true self, on other moments you experience the opposite like disturbed, agitated, not stable, then you are in the grip of the everyday self or ego self. The truth or true self is self-reliant, evolutionary, loving, creative, intelligence, knowing, seeking, accepting, peaceful and pleasantness. The ego self is driven by selfishness, panic, uncertainty, impulsiveness, survival instincts, intellect, power, money and status. I gained a better understanding of how thought and emotion create a conflict between our head and heart. Thought has a certain clarity, whereas with emotion that takes time. The distinction between true self and ego self is the first step to freedom. Understanding how our mind functions, including our intellect, memory, awareness, and ego, enable us to better handle stress and anxiety, through an awareness of Self. Awareness is not something that we do, awareness is what we are.

Our minds are our thoughts, and it is these thoughts that create our world. Nothing else exists. When we sleep without dreams, our so called world doesn't exist. Nothing we have identified with exists: loved ones, work, family, friends, money, favourites, likes and dislikes, everything disappears, until we wake up and open our eyes. This is what our ego mind does, it creates our own unique projection of the world. But what if our thoughts are governed by Ego rather than our True Self? What impact does that have on our view of the world?

Of course, we need the mind to survive, just like any other animal on the planet. But humans who have their basic needs met should be able to access our True Self rather than governed by ego self. All of us are searching, driven by a deep thirst, but so often the water we think we've found turns out to be a mirage. One after the other, we chase mirages, unable to quench our thirst. But what we are looking for is already within us. We are the ocean, and our mind and body are merely a drop of water within it. Once we place our Ego aside and with absolute openness, we will start to see the truth and meaning of life.

The Mind turned inwards is the self, turned outwards it becomes the ego and all the world. The self exists without the mind, never the mind without the self. The Ego self appears and disappears and is transitory, whereas the real self is permanent. Though you are the true self, you wrongly identify the real self with the ego-self. Next time observe in silence how your ego mind is trying to influence your actions, you will start to see the subtle difference of ego-self and the true-self.

The **Tao Te Ching** is a Chinese classic text and foundational work of Taoism. It is central to both philosophical and religious conceptions of Taoism, and had great influence from east to the west, and one of the most translated texts in world literature. The *Tao Te Ching* texts and commentaries date back to two millennia, discovered in ancient bamboo strips, silk threads and paper manuscripts.

Tao means Way or Path, Te means personal character and inner strength, Ching means norm and plan. The *Tao Te Ching* describes the Tao as the source of all existence, it is unseen, but not transcendent, immensely powerful yet supremely humble, being the root of all things. People have desires and free will, and thus are able to alter their own nature. Many act unnaturally upsetting their natural balance of life, so the *Tao Te Ching* intends to lead a person return to their natural state, balance and harmony.

One of the main concepts of *Tao Te Ching* is non action, reflected in multiple meanings like, not doing anything, not forcing, not acting, creating nothingness, acting spontaneously and flowing with the moment. This ancient wisdom will help us to deal with chaotic and busy modern times. It teaches us the way to live with goodness, peace, serenity and integrity.

According to known sources, Lao Tzu was instrumental to Taoism. His teachings reflect an expression of the profound unity of the universe and the path human beings take to join that unity. Here, I will share Lao Tzu quotes from the '*Tao Te Ching*'. For me, the key message is that the truth is one and we all have different paths to get there. These quotes focus on ways to understand life through personal character and inner strength.

The following quotes from different passages of the book 'Tao Te Ching' (Lao Tzu 601 - 531 BC)

Simplicity, Patience, Compassion are your three greatest treasures. Simple in actions and thoughts, you return to the source of being. Patient with both friends and enemies, you accord with the way things are. Compassionate toward yourself, you reconcile all beings in the world.

> Knowing others is intelligence; Knowing yourself is true wisdom.
> Mastering others is strength; Mastering yourself is true power. Conquering others requires force; Conquering one self requires strength.

A man with outward courage dares to die, a man with inner courage dares to live.

The wiseman is one who knows, what he does not know. He who doesn't trust enough, will not be trusted. A man who stands on tiptoe doesn't stand firm.

Ordinary men hate solitude, but the wise makes use of it, embracing his aloneness, realising he is one with the whole universe.

Wise men don't need to prove their point, men who need to prove their point aren't wise.

The master has no possessions, the more he does for others, the happier he is. The more he gives to others, the wealthier he is. The best fighter is never angry. Care about what other people think and you will always be their prisoner.

Best to be like water. Live in a good place. Keep your mind deep. Treat others well. Stand by your word. Keep good order.

Colours blind the eye, sounds deafen the ear, flavours numb the taste, thoughts weaken the mind and desires wither the heart.

Clay is fired to make a pot. The pots use comes from emptiness. Windows and doors are cut to make a room, the rooms use comes from emptiness.

Success is as dangerous as failure; hope is as hollow as fear.

What is firmly rooted cant be pulled out. A violent wind doesn't last for a whole morning, a sudden rain doesn't last for the whole day.

Failure is an opportunity, if you blame someone else, there is no end to the blame. Failure is the foundation of success, and the means by which it is achieved. Therefore, the master fulfils his own obligations and corrects his own mistakes. He does what he needs to do and demands nothings of others.

Trying to understand is like straining through muddy water, have patience to wait, be still and allow the mud to settle. Do you have the patience to wait until your mud settles and the water is clear?

Give evil nothing to oppose and it will disappear by itself. The world belongs to those who let go. When there is no desire, all things are at peace. Rushing into action, you fail. Trying to grasp things, you lose them. Forcing a project to completion, you ruin what was almost ripe. Therefore, the master takes action by letting things take their course. He remains as calm at the end as at the beginning. He has nothing, thus has nothing to lose. What he desires is non desire, what he learns is to unlearn, he simply reminds people of who they have always been. He cares about nothing but the absolute life. Thus, he can care for all things.

A great nation is like a great man, when he makes a mistake, he realises it. Having realised it, he admits it. Having admitted it, he corrects it. He considers those who point out his faults as his most benevolent teachers. He thinks of his enemy as the shadow that he himself casts.

> If you understand others, you are smart, if you understand yourself you are illuminated.
> If you overcome others, you are powerful, if you overcome yourself, you have strength.
> If you know how to be satisfied you are rich,
> If you act with vigour, you have a will.
> If you don't lose your objectives, you can be long lasting,
> If you die without loss, you are eternal.

All streams flow to the sea because it is lower than they are. Be utterly humble and you shall hold to the foundation of peace. Humility gives it its power. If you want to govern the people, you must place yourself below them. If you want to lead the people, you must learn how to follow them.

Stillness is the ruler of movement. Be still like a mountain and flow like a great river. Nature doesn't hurry, yet everything is accomplished. The world is a spiritual vessel and cannot be controlled. Trying to control the world, you won't succeed. Those who control, fail. Those who grasp, lose. If you try to change it, you will ruin it. Try to hold it, and you will lose it.

Weapons are ill-omened tools, not proper instruments. When their use cannot be avoided, calm restraint is best. Don't think they are beautiful, those who think they are beautiful to rejoice in killing people and animals. Those who rejoice in killing cannot achieve their purpose in this world.

Those who know do not speak, those who speak do not know. True words are not eloquent, eloquent words are not true.

When you are in content to be simply yourself and don't compete or compare, everyone will respect you. If you realise that all things change, there is nothing you will try to hold on to. If you are not afraid of death, there is nothing you cannot achieve.

> Watch your thoughts, they become your words.
> Watch your words, they become your actions.
> Watch your actions, they become your habits.
> Watch your habits, they become your character.
> Watch your character, it becomes your destiny.

There is no greater calamity than not knowing what is enough. There is no greater fault than the desire for success. Therefore, knowing that enough is enough is always enough. The further one goes, the less one knows. The flame that burns twice as bright burns half as long.

> If you are depressed, you are living in the past.
> If you are anxious, you are living in the future.
> If you are at peace, you are living in the present.

The truth is not always beautiful, nor beautiful words the truth. Love is a decision, not an emotion. Being deeply loved by someone gives you strength, while loving someone deeply gives you courage. Love of all passions the strongest, for it attacks simultaneously the head, the heart and the senses. Love the world as your own self, then you can truly care for all things. The softest things in the world overcome the hardest things in the world.

> Responsibility without love makes us inconsiderate,
> Power without love makes us cruel,
> Belief without love makes us fanatics,
> Intelligence without love makes us dishonest.
> Kindness in words creates confidence,
> Kindness in thinking creates profoundness,
> Kindness in giving creates love.

The heart that gives, gathers. Love others as much as you love yourself, then you can be entrusted with all things under the heaven. Of all noble qualities, loving compassion is the noblest.

At the centre of your being you have the answer, you know who you are, and you know what you want. When you accept yourself, the whole world accepts you. He who knows others is wise, he who knows himself is enlightened.

A journey of thousand miles begins with a single step.

CHAPTER TWO

Finding Clarity, and the Strength to Follow your Heart

A reflection on knowledge and teachings by authors from around 100 years ago.

Eventually, my family came to accept that my personality didn't fit into Indian society, and my father decided I should move overseas to continue my higher education. He sent many applications on my behalf, and while I was accepted into programmes in Iran, Ukraine, Germany and America, I found ways to avoid going to any of these countries. I needed to make my own decision about my future and wanted to find a country that was geographically far away from my family and less densely populated than what I was used to.

Living in India, a country that's crazy for cricket, meant that I knew about Australia from its record on the pitch. I was more familiar with the cricket grounds in the major Australian cities of Sydney, Melbourne, Brisbane, Adelaide and Perth, such as the SCG Sydney cricket ground, MCG Melbourne cricket ground, the Gabba Brisbane stadium, Adelaide Oval stadium and the WACA Perth stadium – than I was with Australian culture or its Indigenous people. From my school geography classes, I had learned that Australia was the flattest, driest, oldest and largest continent in the world, and of course, I knew about kangaroos and koalas. South Indian cinema at the time filmed many of its songs in Australia, and I felt myself being drawn to the unique beauty of its landscape.

Australia became my first choice. Its distance from India, its smaller population, ticked the boxes for me, true. But I think it was my deepening connection to nature that truly called me to Australia, and I ended up in Sydney.

In the early 2000s, when I was in my twenties, I received three photos of girls in the mail. They were each wearing a saree (a traditional South Indian garment made from a long, unstitched drape), and were posing for the camera with tense, forced smiles. On the back of each photo was the amount their parents were willing to pay in dowry if I agreed to marry them. As the eldest son of an Indian family, I was already under incredible pressure to get married. Arranged marriage is still common in India, driven by tradition and helped by its low divorce rate – less than 5% compared to around 55% in Western countries. The criteria considered when arranging a marriage and calculating a dowry (the amount of property or money given by the bride to her husband on their marriage) are mostly religion, caste, culture, profession, status, horoscope, physical appearance and age. On top of these, skin colour plays a very significant role. I am considered fair-skinned in Southern India, and this helped push up the dowries being offered.

One of the matches was the daughter of a friend of my father. His family was prepared to pay the equivalent of one million Australian dollars in dowry, as well as hand over ownership of their high-end flower business. My parents were keen for me to accept this offer, and to my uncles and family friends, it was a no brainer. Everyone assumed I would accept.

They were shocked when I did not. I was already in a relationship at the time, and it was obvious to my partner and me that my family had no idea who I really was – or they would not have sent the photos in the first place. Most Indian men would have taken the match with the highest dowry and done what their parents expected of them. The most important thing for me, however, was to go with my heart. I remember thinking, 'I can get a bed made of pure gold, but not a peaceful or pleasant sleep'. Not for a moment did I consider choosing money and status over freedom.

The process of making that decision and going against the interests of my family taught me to be strong enough to follow my heart. Freedom means being able to reject the leadership of the majority. I learned that each of us are unique, we are individual, and that knowing our True Self is a part of our purpose in life. But then, in 2004, my mother died. She was fifty years old.

At the time, I hadn't seen my family or visited India for almost four years. No one had told me anything about my mother feeling unwell, or the many tests being done on a lump detected in her throat. Oblivious, I returned to India to attend my sister's wedding and was devastated by what I found. My mother had lost so much weight, she was only skin and bones. Tears in my eyes, speechless from shock, my entire world ground to a sudden halt. I felt none of the heat and humidity of Chennai, hardly even noticed the chaos and crowds of the city. All I saw, all I felt, all that mattered, was my mother. Slowly, my family revealed the truth to me. She had been diagnosed with throat cancer.

After the wedding, I took my mother on many trips from the town of Nellore to a cancer treatment hospital in Chennai in a desperate bid to extend her life. It was a three to four-hour journey each way. The doctors told me that the cancer was in a late-stage, and she had less than six months to live. Heartbroken, I searched for answers and finally came across a doctor who was willing to operate. He could remove the lump, he said, and she might live another ten years, but she could lose her voice in the process.

All I wanted was for my mother to live, just long enough so I could bring her to Sydney and show her a slice of my new life in Australia. I know now, how selfish I was being. But she was my mother, and I loved her.

My mother didn't like the idea of going through with the operation, especially after the chemotherapy she'd already endured. But I was her son, and for me, she agreed to do it. I believe she had already resigned herself to death, and only agreed to the operation to make me happy. I returned to Sydney, promising I'd be back to help her through her operation and recovery. But before I could return, her operation was brought forward. My family lived four hours away and could not be there with her. Luckily, a childhood friend of mine, who was well-known by my family and lived in Chennai, was kind enough to be by her side. Through my friend, I spoke to the doctors and nurses, learning that her operation was successful – but she had lost her voice as feared. With his help, I told my mother that I would see her in a few weeks, as I had already organised to head back to India.

My friend recalls that my mother used sign language to ask for an image of her favourite god, and then thanked him with her hands. An hour later, she was in a coma.

Some twenty-four to forty-eight hours after I called my mother from Sydney, I was advised of her condition. I managed to book a flight that night, landed in Chennai and went directly to the hospital. Later that day, despite the efforts of the doctors, she passed away. I organised an ambulance – more like a van, really – to take my mother's body from Chennai to our village for her burial rites. It was a four-hour journey. I remember holding her hand and touching her forehead, but all I could feel was the coldness of her skin. The reality that she was no longer in her body sunk into me with that feeling.

My mother passed away in 2004, by 2005 my family had pressured me into marriage. I would call it emotional blackmail – I felt like I was left with no choice but to comply with their wishes. So, in June of that year, I took my partner – who is Caucasian – to India to introduce her to my family. Despite the cultural differences and the difficulties of the situation, my partner was very supportive. She understood that we were going through tough times and tried to see it from the perspective of Indian tradition and culture. We got married in India, and our marriage was so unusual that we were featured in the local newspaper and even interviewed for television. A man with a camera approached us, without warning, and began to ask questions: 'What do you think about inter-caste marriage?' 'How do your pa rents feel about this?' 'Do your parents agree with your decision to marry a foreign girl?' We answered as best we could, saying that our parents from both sides had agreed and were happy with the marriage. I honestly hadn't given it much thought, especially with everything already going on in my life and in my mind. It was surreal to have so much attention on me, just because I was marrying a white woman from the West.

In 2008, my father was diagnosed with mouth cancer. Luckily, it was diagnosed early, and with chemotherapy, he managed to survive. It took him a good twelve months from diagnosis to recovery. But this is the nature of life; it presents us with unforeseen challenges, and it is up to us to make the most of every situation. My brother took good care of my father during those times, as I was occupied with my own life challenges.

Life experiences taught me especially with experiences in India, that despite appearances, all beings and things are interconnected and fundamentally one. When an individual is not awake to the essential truth, then the person sees themselves as separate and isolated from the world around them. The greatest illusion in the world is the illusion of separation. The illusion of separation is what continues to keep us away from our authentic self and experiencing the oneness. Separation is the root of all evil.

The chaos we see in society today reflects the chaos within us. If we wish to heal society, we need to heal ourselves. Our society and the people within it operate on a world view that is based on separation. The separation between mind and body, seen and unseen, physical and non-physical is the root of all evil.

Separation and inequality still exist, in the name of caste, culture, faith and religion. Even as a teenager, I wanted to understand why. When I dared ask the question as a kid, I was told 'it's god's will', or 'it's because they did evil in a previous life'. But driven by my curiosity and already beginning to think independently, I simply could not accept these vague answers, and so began a quest for understanding. A journey towards the truth.

In my teenage years, I invested a lot of time trying to understand faith and religion. I studied Hinduism, Christianity, Islam, Buddhism, Jainism and other mainstream faiths. The more I read, the more I learned, the more I started to realise that all religions are simply different paths towards a single truth. Not only did I read as many texts as I could get my hands on, but I was lucky to connect to others who helped me on my way.

Separation exists mainly with what we identify with, our Intellect which is Buddhi Gets identified with something, and you function within the world of this identity. Whatever you are identified with, all your thoughts and emotions spring from that identity. If you don't restrict your intellect with any identifications such as body, gender, family, qualifications, society, race, creed, community & nation, then you travel naturally toward your ultimate nature.

It is in our nature we are one big cosmic family and by laws of universe, which can further understand about gender identity and oneness. Majority of us identify with gender and physicality, and feel divisive, inferior or superior, good or bad by comparison. From the universal law of gender, we learn about masculine and feminine energies. These energies are not based on physicality, but we all carry both. Because of the way we are raised in our societies, most individuals are never able to balance these energies.

Universal Law of Gender says Everything has its masculine Yang and feminine Yin principles and are the basis for all creation. The spiritual initiate must balance the Yang and Yin energies within herself or himself to become a master. Gender is not limited to physical appearance. This is the law that governs creation and in its simplest understanding states that everything in nature is both male and female. Both are required equally for life to exist. No one is greater or lesser than the other and both sides are inhabited within everyone irrespective of whether one is male or female. The law of oneness says everything is connected.

Universal Law of Oneness is that We live in a world where everything is connected to everything else. Everything we do, say, think and believe affects others and the universe around us. Energy is everything all at once and it flows through everything living or inanimate. We will see our own reflection in the people and things around us. It means that the better we think about others, the better it comes back to us and become us.

A limited identity that we impose upon ourselves is what sets us up as Me versus the Others. It is in this space of division and separation that all the negativity is born.

When you ask another human being, 'who are you?' the answer is usually something they have identified with, a name, title, ethnicity, country, status, power etc. Not many would know the true answer. We live in a society and a world where most of us aren't guided to a deeper understanding of 'who I am'. Our strong attachment to worldly things, the way we use them to create our identity, can make it difficult to reach an understanding of the True Self. Hence, we live in a world of separation. In other words, by ruling out the things that we strongly identify ourselves with, like our name, title, position, power, money, brother, sister, mother, father, children, religion, caste, creed, race, ideology, place, city, country, sports team and so on, we will get closer to our True Self or oneness.

The greatest illusion in this world is the illusion of separation, in one moment you perceive one image as ugly and, in another view, you may see same image as good. Look again through different eyes and you will see a beautiful image. We may readily see the separation or divisiveness, but then we can marvel at the view of the earth from the moon, seeing a breathtaking beautiful blue green floating earth as oneness. We are all connected through the common thread that is our universal consciousness. However, we don't always naturally feel this inter connection in our day-to-day life, mainly due to the illusion of separation. We live in our own reality where everything appears separate, especially with our physical appearances. But beneath our physical body, emotions, thoughts lie our consciousness. Since we don't know what others are thinking and their emotions, we assume and act as if consciousness is ours alone, as if consciousness stops at our skin and physical appearances. It is no fault of anyone to think this way, as we all have been conditioned to think this way. The illusion of separation has an impact on our lives in this physical world or day to day reality, which leads to how we think and act with ourselves and others.

We are all one. There is no separation. Separation is an illusion of the dualistic mind, where our mind is conditioned to choose between two sides. When we are afraid of our true nature, we cling onto labels, false identification and standards to feel certainty & belonging. We are endlessly caught in the cycle of the illusion and separation with what we identify with. From childhood, we are taught that the world is divided into sides, into likes and dislikes, into good and bad, into self and other. This influences the way we see the world. But separation is an illusion. As a flower blossoms with sunshine, earth, gardener, water and so on, yet you see only beautiful flower and no other elements which contributed for the flower to blossom. We are far more connected to everything in the cosmos than we could possibly imagine. And there is hope in that connection.

If I am asked to recommend one book which summarises life in a simple and easy to read way (and in under fifty pages) it would be *The Prophet*. This book helped me when I was still processing the guilt I felt about the circumstances around my mother's death.

All decisions are made under some measure of emotional and social pressure, but I couldn't help feeling uneasy about how I handled the situation. *The Prophet* helped me understand the true meaning of death, marriage, relationships and love. It challenged me to rethink what I believed I knew about my parents, society, schooling, work – in fact, so many aspects of life. It helped me flush out all I had been taught, and see life from a fresh, new perspective, one that contradicted a lot of what society and culture take for granted. Because of this, I am now more at peace with the past, and no longer let it exert undue influence on my present.

The Prophet is the story of a wise man, who sets sail for his homeland after twelve years in exile. He is asked to share his wisdom on the big questions in life. I have summarised my notes from the book in the next few pages. This book speaks of love, marriage, children, giving, eating and drinking, work, sorrow, houses, clothes, buying and selling, crime and punishment, laws, freedom, reason and passion, pain, self-knowledge, teaching, friendship, talking, time, good and evil, prayer, pleasure, beauty, religion and death. The following quotes from the book *The Prophet* by Kahlil Gibran.

Love - Gives nothing but itself and takes nothing but from itself. Love possesses not nor would it be possessed. For love is sufficient to love. If you love somebody, let them go, for if they return, they were always yours. If they don't, they never were. Love knows not its own depth until the hour of separation. Love without love is like a tree without blossoms of fruit. Love has no other desire but to fulfil itself.

Marriage - Love one another but make not a bond of love. Sing and dance together and be joyous but let each one of you be alone. Fill each other's cup but drink not from one cup. Give one another of your bread but not eat from same loaf. Give your hearts but not into each other's keeping. Let there be spaces in your togetherness. And let the winds of the heavens dance between you. Let it be a moving sea between the shores of your souls.

Children - Your children are not your children. They are the sons and daughters of life's longing for itself, they come through you but not from you. You may give them your love but not your thoughts, for they have their own thoughts. You may house their bodies but not their souls, for their soul's dwell in the house of tomorrow, which you cannot visit, not even in your dreams. You may strive to be like them but seek not to make them like you. You are the bows from which your children as living arrows are sent forth.

Giving – It is well to give when asked, but it is better to give unasked, through understanding. You would give, but only to the deserving, the trees in your orchard say not so, nor the flocks in the pasture. See first that you yourself deserve to be a giver, and an instrument of giving. You give but little when you give of your possessions. It is when you give of yourself that you truly give. For in truth, it is the life that gives to life while you who dream yourself a giver, are but a witness.

Work - To love life through labour is to be intimate with life's inmost secret. Work is love made visible. And if you cannot work with love but only with distaste, it is better that you should leave your work and sit at the gate of the temple and take alms of those who work with joy. For if you bake bread with indifference, you bake a bitter bread that feeds but half man's hunger. Work with love is to weave the cloth with threads drawn from your heart, as if your beloved were to wear that cloth. It is to build a house with affection, as if your beloved were to dwell in that house. It is to sow seeds with tenderness and reap the harvest with joy, as if your beloved were to eat the fruit. It is to charge all things you fashion with a breath of your own spirit. In keeping yourself with labour you are in truth loving life. You work that you may keep pace with the earth and the soul of the earth. When you work with love you bind yourself to yourself and to one another and to God.

Joy and Sorrow - Your joy is your sorrow unmasked. They are inseparable the deeper that sorrow is carved into your being the more joy you can contain. When you are sorrowful look again in your heart, and you shall see that in truth you are weeping for that which has been your delight. The deeper that sorrow carves into your being, the more joy you can contain.

House - Your house is your larger body. What is it you guard with fastened doors? Peace, beauty, remembrances or comfort which enters the house a guest, then becomes a host, and then a master. And it becomes a tamer, and with hook and scourge makes puppets of your life desires. Though of magnificence and splendour, your house shall not hold your secret nor shelter your longing. Your house shall be not an anchor but a mast. It shall not be a glistening film that covers a wound, but an eyelid that guards the eye.

Clothes - Your clothes conceal much of your beauty, yet they hide not the unbeautiful. And though you seek in garments the freedom of privacy you may find in them a harness and a chain.

Crime and Punishment – It is when your spirit goes wandering upon the wind, that you alone and unguarded, commit a wrong unto others and therefore unto yourself. You cannot separate the just from unjust and the good from wicked, for they stand together before the face of the sun even as the black thread and the white woven together. What judgement pronounce upon who though honest in the flesh yet is a thief in spirit. The cornerstone of the temple is not higher than the lowest stone in its foundation.

Freedom – You can only be free when even the desire of seeking freedom becomes a harness to you, and when you cease to speak of freedom as a goal and a fulfilment. You shall be free indeed when your days are not without a care nor your nights without a want and a grief, but rather when these things girdle your life and yet you rise above them naked and unbound.

Reason and Passion – Your reason and your passion are the rudder and the sails of your own seafaring soul. If either of your sails or rudder be broken, you can but toss and drift or else be held at a standstill in mid seas. For reason, ruling alone, is a force confining and passion, unattended, is a flame that burns to its own destruction. Let your soul direct your passion with reason, that your passion may live through its own daily resurrection and the phoenix rise above its own ashes. Your soul is oftentimes a battlefield, upon your reason and your judgement wage war against your passion and your appetite.

Pain and suffering - Your pain is the breaking of the shell that encloses your understanding. Much of your pain is self-chosen. It is the bitter potion by which the physician within you heals your sick self. Therefore, trust the physician, and drink his remedy in silence and tranquillity, for his hand, though heavy and hard, guided by the tender hand of unseen, and the cup he brings, though it burns your lips, has been fashioned of the clay which the potter has moistened with his own scared tears. Out of suffering have emerged the strongest souls, the most massive characters are seared with scars.

Friendship - Your friend is your needs answered. He/she is your field which you sow with love and reap with thanksgiving. For it is his/her to fill your need, but not your emptiness. In the sweetness of friendship let there be laughter and sharing of pleasures. For in the dew of little things, does the heart find its morning and is refreshed.

Talking - You talk when you cease to be at peace with your thoughts. And when you can no longer dwell in the solitude of your heart you live in your lips, and sound is a diversion and a pastime. And in much of your talking, thinking is half murdered.

Good and Evil - You are good when you are not one with yourself. Yet when you are not one with yourself you are not evil. You are good when you strive to give of yourself. Yet you are not evil when you seek gain for yourself. You are good when you are fully awake in your speech. Yet you are not evil when you sleep while your tongue staggers without purpose. You are good when you walk to your goal firmly and with bold steps. Yet you are not evil when you go there limping. You are good in countless ways, and you are not evil when you are not good.

Pleasure - Pleasure is a freedom song sing it with the fullness of heart, yet don't lose your heart in the singing. Your hearts know in silence the secrets of the days and the nights. The lust for comfort kills the passions of the soul. The pleasure of the bee to gather honey of the flower is also the pleasure of the flower to yield its honey to the bee. For to the bee a flower is a fountain of life, and to the flower a bee is a messenger of love, and to both, the bee and the flower, the giving and receiving of pleasure is a need and an ecstasy. Be in your pleasures like the flowers and the bees.

Beauty - Beauty is life when life unveils her holy face, but you are life, and you are the veil. Beauty is eternity gazing at itself in a mirror. But you are eternity, and you are the mirror. Beauty is not the image you would see nor the song you would hear, but rather an image you see though you close your eyes and a song you hear though you shut your ears.

Religion - Your daily life is your temple and your religion. I love you when you bow in your mosque, kneel in your temple, pray in your church. For you and I are sons of one religion, and it is the spirit.

Death - You would know the secret of death, but how shall you find it unless you seek it in the heart of life. For life and death are one, even as the river and the sea are one. Death is to stand naked in the wind and to melt into the sun. Cease breathing is to free the breath from its restless tides, that it may rise and expand and seek God unburdened. Only when you drink from the river of silence shall you indeed sing. And when you have reached the mountain top, then you shall begin to climb. And when the earth shall claim your limbs, then shall you truly dance.

Don't forget that earth delights to feel your bare feet and the winds long to play with your hair. The timeless in you is aware of life's timelessness. And knows that yesterday is but today's memory and tomorrow is today's dream.

Self is a sea boundless and measureless.

Siddhartha is more popular in the Western world than the Eastern world, so I came across this book at a later stage in my life. When I was growing up in India, Buddhism and Buddha appeared often in storytelling. Siddhartha Gautama commonly referred as the buddha meaning the awakened was born to royal parents and lived in south Asia during 6th or 5th century BC. He lived among the luxuries of the palace, was married, had a son, and had everything as a royal family. Only after his experience with four signs, the old age, sickness, death and contentment, he understood that everyone he loved, every fine object, all his grand clothes, his horses, his jewels and wealth would one day be lost subject to age, illness and death. This idea of tremendous loss became unbearable to him, but he noticed an ascetic seemed at peace and content. He learned from the ascetic there is a path of spiritual reflection, detachment, and recognising the world of illusions. One night after looking at the precious objects he was attached to and his sleeping wife and son, he walked out of the palace, with no possessions in search of enlightenment. He became a prince who renounced his position and wealth to live a wandering ascetic seeking enlightenment. He was born during a time of social and religious transformation when several thinkers had begun to question the authority of the priests and misuse of the ancient scriptures. Buddha represents an enlightened person who can live life by separating the True Self from the mind and body. Our pain and suffering are mostly caused by the mind and body. An enlightened person can control their mind and body, rather than allow themselves to be controlled. He introduced in his first sermon the four noble truths, Life is suffering, the cause of suffering is craving, the end of suffering comes with an end to craving, there is a path which leads one away from craving and suffering. One can enjoy all aspects of life like a dinner party, when the meal is done, one tanks one's host for the pleasant time and goes home. One doesn't start crying and feeling depressed lamenting the evening end. The nature of dinner party is that it has a beginning and an ending, it is not a permanent state, and neither is anything else in life. Instead of mourning the loss of something that one could never hope to have held onto, one should appreciate what one has experienced for what it is and let it go when it is over.

I read *Siddhartha* as an adult and understood from it that the world is not imperfect, or on a slow path towards perfection; no, it is perfect in every moment. What we see or perceive as good or bad is all a part of life, and we need to accept that as truth.

We don't need to leave our so-called 'normal' life and go to the Himalayas or become a hermit, to attain peace and pleasantness. Sin, lust, desire, vanity, and despair are necessary: they teach us how to open a path to loving life as it is and stop comparing it to some imagined or wished-for world. My own experiences include lust, desire, sin, and pain, and they have helped motivate me to understand the root causes and begin the pursuit of pleasantness in my life.

Knowledge can be conveyed, but not wisdom. Knowledge (truth) can be found, it can be lived, it is possible to be carried by it, miracles can be performed with it, but it cannot be expressed in words and taught. The opposite of every truth is just as true! That's like this; Any truth can only be expressed and put into words when it is one-sided. Everything is one-sided which can be thought with thoughts and said with words, it's all one-sided, all just one half, all lacks completeness, roundness, oneness.

Buddha and his disciples were constantly moving from village to village and from town to town. Wherever he went, he had at least 2000 to 3000 monks with him. These were all people who beg for their food and eat. India is a culture where if a spiritual person comes to your door and asks for food, even if your own children have not eaten, you must first give it to him. When people were like this, every time he entered a town with 100 - 200 monks, suddenly there would be a pressure on the villagers. So he made a rule that they should never stay in any place for more than three days so as to not burden the people.

Only during the monsoons, it would be very difficult to travel by foot through the jungles because the northern and eastern part of the Indian subcontinent receives heavy rains. Walking through the jungles would have been treacherous, and many would have lost their lives. Therefore, this was a time when they stayed in a larger town and spread across many homes.

During the day, the monks went out for alms. One of the monks encountered a courtesan. She gave him alms, looked at him, a tall and handsome young man, and said, "I heard that monks are looking for shelter. Why don't you come and stay in my house?" Monk said, "I must ask the Buddha as to where I should stay." She became really taunting, "Oh, you want to ask your Guru? Go and ask him. Let's see what he says." Monk went back to Buddha and put what he had collected at his feet. Everyone was supposed to find food and shelter wherever they go. So Monk asked, "This lady is inviting me. Can I stay there?" Buddha said, "If she is inviting you, you must go and stay there." Upon hearing that, the townspeople who were around were up in arms. They said, "What? A monk is going to stay at a prostitute's home. This is it! This spiritual process has become corrupt." Buddha looked at them and said, "Why are you so worried? The lady is inviting him. Let him stay there. What is the problem?"

People started to get up. He said, "Wait. I am on this path because I see that this is the most precious and powerful way to live. Now you are telling me that her ways are more powerful than mine? If that was the truth, I should go and join her. As a seeker of truth if you find something much higher, you should go for that." People were in high dudgeon, and of course, many left. Monk went and stayed with her. Because of the rains, it got cold. He was only wearing a thin robe, so she gave him a nice silk wrap. He covered himself with it. When people saw this, they took it as evidence that he was going astray. She cooked nice food for him.

He ate. In the evening, she danced for him. He sat watching with utmost attention. When people heard the music, they thought he had fallen. Time passed. When the rains stopped and it was time to move on, Monk came to Buddha with a female monk. This is the power of being on the path of truth.

Buddha after being enlightenment spoke in his teachings of the world, he had to divide it into Sansara and Nirvana. Into deception and truth. Into suffering and salvation. It can't be done differently, there is no other way for him who wants to teach. But the world itself, what exists around us and inside us, is never one-sided. Opinions mean nothing, they may be beautiful or ugly, clever or foolish, anyone can embrace or reject them.

A person or an act is never entirely sansara or entirely nirvana, A person is never entirely holy or entirely sinful. It does really seem like this, because we are subject to deception as if time was something real. Time is not real, and if time is not real, then the gap which seems to be between the world and the eternity, between suffering and blissfulness, between evil and good, is also a deception. It is not for me to judge another man's life. I must judge, I must choose, I must reject, purely for myself. For myself alone.

The world is not imperfect, or on a slow path towards perfection; no it is perfect in every moment. All sin already carries the divine forgiveness, all small children already have the old person in themselves, all infants already have death, all dying people the eternal life. It may be important to great thinkers to examine the world, to explain and despise it. But it is important to love the world, not to despise it, but to be able to regard the world and us and all beings with love, admiration and respect.

It is not possible for any person to see how far another one has already progressed on his/her path, in the robber and gambler the Buddha is waiting; in the Buddha, the robber is waiting.

In deep meditation, there is the possibility to put time out of existence, to see all life which was, is and will be as if it was simultaneously, and there everything is good, everything is perfect. Therefore, we need to see whatever exists as good, Death is like life, Sin like holiness, Wisdom like foolishness.

Everything must be as it is, everything only requires our consent, our willingness, our loving agreement to be good for us, to do nothing but work for our benefit, to be unable to ever harm us. We need sin, lust, desire, vanity and despair in order to learn how to give up all resistance, in order to learn how to love the world, in order to stop comparing it to some world you wished, imagined, some kind of perfection you made up, but to leave it as it is and to love it and enjoy being a part of it.

Life is like a river. The river is everywhere. At the source, at the mouth, at the waterfall, at the current, in the ocean and in the mountains, all at the same time as present and not the shadow of the past nor the shadow of the future. We learn from the river how to listen, to listen with a still heart, with waiting, open soul, without passion, without desire, without judgements and without opinions. Water is the voice of life, the voice of being, the voice of becoming. Within you, there is a stillness and a sanctuary to which you can retreat at anytime and be yourself. A true seeker, one who truly wished to find truth, could accept no doctrine. But the man who had found what he sought, such a man could approve of every doctrine, each and every one, every path, every goal, nothing separates him any longer from all those thousands of others who lived the eternal and breathed the divine.

One must find the source within one's own self. Your soul is the whole world.

When we see ourselves as different from the world, the inequality and biasness exist. We will face inequality at some point in life, some more than others. If poverty, injustice, discrimination and gross inequality persist in our world, none of us can truly attain peace and see life as fair. I have faced my own share of inequality, I will share some of those experiences, I was looking to rent a place in this well-known metropolitan city, I was rejected several times based on my skin colour and ethnicity. The property manager and the owner said, this property is not for Indian ethnicity. Even though I had money, clean character and in a good high paid job, I was discriminated based on biasness. Strange world we live in, that's all I thought at that moment. My wife is Caucasian with pale skin colour, and the nasty comments I got in my face being with her on the streets wasn't nice either. Horrible things were said and sometimes just the body language of others, the way they express is close to disgust and not approving on what I am living, or who I am with or what they are seeing.

But the inequality and discrimination I faced since childhood, didn't bother me. I knew those individuals are discriminating based on their limited identity either consciously or unconsciously. The fear and insecurity within themselves are the root cause of their actions against others. When I was young, I was deeply uneasy about the inequality I saw around me: between rich and poor, between genders, based on skin colour and culture. During school summer holidays at home, I was not allowed to help my mother in the kitchen because I was the eldest son. I was told it is a female place and I should not participate. Very strange for me that spending time with my mother had society rules. On the other hand, If I expressed a desire to help the less fortunate, I was told that God was punishing them for their sins and instructed to do nothing. It confused me to the core and felt helpless myself. When I was a kid, as simple a thing as visiting a tea shop in my village was, in my view, plagued by prejudice, and injustice. Lower caste customers were seated on the floor and served tea in glass cups, which they then had to wash. Members of the upper caste drunk tea at a bench, from steel mugs. With recent years of road extensions its fortunate that the tea shop no longer exists and the discrimination in the minds still exists. Other incidents which left a mark on me when I was young, and still play in my head and my heart, are reports I read in the newspaper when I was in my pre-teens. A low caste man was held in captivity, tortured, and forced to consume human faeces and urine, all because he had an affair with a high caste girl. Low caste girls, on the other hand, were either forced to walk naked in front of other villagers or sexually abused for not following high caste rules. Incidents like these are quite common to this day and age in lot of countries and have only recently started appearing in Western media due to the activity of social media.

    This Separation and inequality still exist, in the name of caste, culture, skin colour, social status, class, race and religion. When we ask ourselves deeply WHY, the immediate answer I get is we are all bought up to be biased. We are conditioned to look after our own versus others. This bias and prejudice, or simply ignorance, can lead to isolation, vulnerability, disadvantage and discrimination at school, at work, in stores, on streets and other services, or even where people live impacting humanity across all stages of life. On top of that the causes of social inequality include society's acceptance of roles, stereotyping, social organisation by class or caste system, economic disparity as well as political inequality. According to United Nations, Today, wherever people live, they don't have to look far to confront inequalities. Inequality in its various forms is an issue that will define our time. Confronting inequalities has moved to the forefront of many global policy debates as an agreement has emerged that all should enjoy equal access to opportunity. Inequalities are not only driven and measured by income, but are determined by other factors - gender, age, origin, ethnicity, disability, sexual orientation, class, and religion. These factors determine inequalities of opportunity which continue to persist, within and between countries. In some parts of the world, these divides are becoming more pronounced. Meanwhile, gaps in newer areas, such as access to online and mobile technologies are emerging. Groups such as indigenous peoples, migrants and refugees, and ethnic and other minorities continue to suffer from discrimination, marginalisation, and lack of legal rights. This is pervasive across developing and developed countries alike and is not tied to income. The result is a complex mix of internal and external challenges that will continue to grow over the next twenty-five years. We have to wait and see if we are really moving towards humanity where everyone feels equal and have a voice.

We are great with sympathy but not empathy in our actions. There is huge difference between the two, were we often get confused. Empathy means experiencing someone else's feelings and shown in how much compassion and understanding we can give to another. Sympathy, on the other hand, means understanding someone else's suffering. It is more of a feeling of pity for another. Empathy leads to actions while sympathy is easily forgotten. One way we can tackle this inequality on a personal level is by simply accepting everyone for who they are without judging and treating others as our own part of being. Thats our true nature and in that true nature there is inclusion, joy and oneness. Inequality exists in our minds, in our biases and prejudices, and that remains to be fixed. We need to challenge our own mindset and shift to achieve equality.

The Book of Mirdad presents a series of dialogues between Mirdad, the abbot of a monastery built where Noah's Ark came to rest after the flood subsided, and his disciples. These dialogues occurred when the disciple Naronda was admitted as a servant in the monastery. His teachings cover important life issues such as love, the master-servant relationship, creative silence, money, the moneylender and the debtor, the cycle of time and death, repentance, and old age. The discussion calls for the unity of different groups of people to achieve universal love and criticises materialism and empty religious rituals. From this book, I learned how to transform consciousness and uncover the god within by dissolving our sense of duality. I connected well with the characters as accessible representations of our societies and communities. I found myself embodied by one of the characters in each conversation and situation.

In *The Book of Mirdad* each character has a name that carries meaning, symbolising universal characteristics within each person. These names are easily pronounced in any language and add a touch of antiquity without identifying too much with any particular era or race. 'Mirdad', for example, is taken from an Arabic root that means 'to return' – the man who comes back again and again as an Avatar. 'Shamadam' is combination of two English names Sham and Adam – the false man. 'Micayon' is constructed from Jewish name Mikhail meaning he who is like god. 'Micaster' is star-like. 'Zamora' comes from an Arabic root meaning playing a musical instrument. 'Bennoon' is the noon sun, noon being a letter of the Arabic alphabet that relates to a judge and logician. 'Himbal' is suggestive of Baal, meaning Idol worship. 'Naronda' is a sonorous name suggestive of truth, honesty, and devotion. 'Abimar' is chosen for its melodiousness, 'Mar' being suggestive of distrust. This book reads along the same lines as 'The Prophet', with a surface narrative that is easy to follow, but rich with deeper dialogues and meaning.

The following quotes from different passages of *The Book of Mirdad* by Mikhail Naimy

> Die to live; Live to die. Speech is at best an honest lie. While silence is at worst a naked truth.

> The truly high is ever low; The truly swift is ever slow
> The highly sensitive is numb; The highly eloquent is dumb
> The ebb and flow are but one tide; The guideless has the surest guide
> The very great is very small and he has all who gives his all.

> Should you find the waiting long, it shall be made longer. Should you find it short, it shall be made shorter. Believe and be patient.

> Accept misfortune as if it were a fortune. For a misfortune once understood is soon transformed into a fortune. While a

fortune misconstrued quickly becomes a misfortune. The poor is he who misuses what he has. The rich is he who well uses what he has.

Vast is the difference between holding and being held. You hold only what you love, what you hate holds you. Avoid being held.

Ask not of things to shed their veils. Unveil yourselves and things will be unveiled. Often you shall think your road impassable, sombre and companionless. Have will and plod along, and round each curve you shall find a new companion.

Love is the law of God. You live that you may learn to love. You love that you may learn to live. No other lesson is required of man. You are the tree of life. Beware of breaking yourselves. Set not a fruit against fruit, a leaf against a leaf, a branch against a branch; nor set the stem against the roots, nor set the tree against the mother soil. That is precisely what you do when you love one part more than the rest, or to the exclusion of the rest.

Love is the only freedom from attachment. When you love everything, you are attached to nothing. No love is possible except by the love of self.

No love is love that controls the lover. No love is love that feeds on flesh and blood. No love is love that draws a woman to a man only to breed more women and men and thus perpetuate their bondage to the flesh.

Whoever cannot find a temple in his/her heart, the same can never find his heart in any temple.

The servant is the master's master; The master is the servant's servant.

Let not the servant bow his head, let not the master raise it high.

Crush out the deadly master's pride, root out the shameful servant's shame.

A tree can spread no further than its roots. While humans can spread unto infinity, for he/she is rooted in eternity. Set no limits to yourselves. Spread out until there are no regions where you are not. Spread out until the whole world be wherever you may chance to be. This is the way to freedom from care and pain.

The key to life is the creative word; The key to creative word is love; The key to love is understanding. Once understanding is unveiled, then victory is won, and peace established in the heart for ever. An understanding heart is ever at peace even amid a war dazed world. An ignorant heart is a dual heart. A dual heart makes a dual world. A dual world breeds constant strife and war. Whereas an understanding heart is a single heart. A single heart makes a single world. A single world is a world at peace. For it takes two to make a war.

There are no halts and starts in time. Time is a continuity, which overlaps itself nothing is ended and dismissed in time, and nothing is begun and dismissed. Time is a wheel created by the senses, and by the senses set a whirling in the voids of space. You sense the bewildering change of seasons, and you believe, therefore that all is in the clutches of change. The law of time is repetition. What once occurred in time is bound to reoccur again and again, the intervals in the case of humans may be long or brief depending on the intensity of each person desire and will for repetition. Time is the universal memory. There are no accidents in time and space.

Accept all the things that fall to you, in gratitude.

The wheel of time revolves around the voids of space. Upon the rim are all the things perceivable by the senses, which are unable to perceive a thing except in time and space. So things continue to appear and disappear. What disappears for one at a certain point of time and space appears for another at another point. One is the road of life and death. If the growth be the child of decay, and decay be the child of growth; if the life be the mother of death, and death be the mother of life, then truly they but one at every point of time and space. The wheel of time rotated but it's axis at rest. Let time revolve about you, but you revolve not with time.

Everything has will. It's a consciousness of willingness and of being that may differ in degree from that of humans, but not in substance. You equipped with brains and memories and means of recording emotions and thoughts, are yet an unconscious major part of a single day's living. The creation is conscious of your unconsciousness and that of every creature in the universe. Be mindful of how you breathe, and how you speak and what you wish, think, and do. For your Will is hid in every breath, every word, every wish, thought and deed. And what is hid from you is always manifest to the existence/universe.

Don't will of any person a pleasure that is to he/she a pain, avoid your pleasure-pain you more than pain. Nor will of anything a good that is to it an evil, avoid you be willing evil to yourselves. Till you grow conscious of all things you cannot be conscious of their will in you, nor your will in them. Till you are conscious of your will in all things and of their will in you, you cannot know the mysteries of the universe.

A dreadful burden is of old age to humans as well as to animals. Upon a newborn they lavish their utmost care and affection. But to an age burdened they reserve their indifference more than their care and their disgust more than their sympathy. The very young and the very old are equally helpless. But truly the old are more deserving of sympathy than the young.

Examine well your heads. Would you be rulers of men and women? Learn first to rule yourselves. How else can you rule well except you be well self-ruled. Humans are full of tumult, anarchy and chaos. If you truly govern humans, dive to their utmost depths. But to dive to the utmost depths, you must first dive to your own utmost depths. All world authority, whatever be its source is counterfeit. Because of their lust for authority humans are in constant turmoil. Those in authority are ever struggling to snatch it from the hands of those who hold it or ever fighting to maintain it. The world is poor, so poor to understand, therefore it seeks to hide its poverty behind the veil of counterfeit authority.

No authority is worth the flutter of an eyelash, except the authority of holy understanding which is priceless. For that no sacrifice is great. Attain it once, and you shall hold it to the end of time. And it shall charge your words with more power than all the armies of the world can ever command, and it shall bless your deeds with more beneficence than all the world authorities combined can ever dream of bringing to the world.

Yes fight, but not your neighbour. Fight rather all the things that cause you and your neighbour to fight. Why does anyone wish to fight you, is it because your eyes are blue, and his/her eyes are hazel; is it because you dream of angels, and he/she dreams of the devil; is it because you are white, and they are dark-skinned or is it because you love them as yourself and hold all yours as theirs. If nothing else can make you feel your oneness with the universe, the earth alone should make you feel it. Rub your eyes and be awake. For you are more than earth. Your destiny is more than to live and die and provide abundant food for the ever-hungry jaws of death. Your destiny is to be free from living and from dying and all the warring opposites incumbent on duality.

Can the eye see all to be seen and the ear hear all to be heard, can the hand feel all to be felt, the nose smell all to be smelled or can the tongue taste all to be tasted. Only when faith born of divine imagination, comes to their aid will the senses truly sense and thus become ladders to the summit. Senses devoid of pure imagination faith are most undependable guides.

Less possessing less possessed; More possessing more possessed.

More possessed less accessed; Less possessed more accessed.

A beautiful story about a bird, cat and poop teaches us on how to perceive life. A little bird was flying during a cold snowstorm. It was so cold that the bird couldn't fly anymore and fell and landed near some barn. While lying down helpless on the ground, a cow came by and dropped a big poop on her. The poop was so warm that the little freezing bird started warming up and feeling better. The bird was so happy to feel warm that she started to sing. A cat heard the bird singing, so he followed the voice until he found the bird, so he dug her out of the poop and ate her. The morals of the story: Not everybody who shits on you is your enemy. Not everybody who digs you out of the shit is your friend. When you're in deep shit, keep quiet.

When I was a student, I worked at a service station in Woolloomooloo, near Kings Cross and close to Sydney's CBD. My shift started on Friday night and finished on Sunday morning. No one else wanted to do this shift (which was famously called the graveyard shift). In those days, Kings Cross was full of strip clubs, drag queens, pimps, drug dealers and addicts, buskers, artists, partygoers, and con artists. It overflowed with the promise of forbidden pleasure, but it was also a place of danger, especially at night. I used to get the train to Kings Cross station and walk the backstreets towards Woolloomooloo. Most of my colleagues had bad experiences: some were held at gunpoint, others threatened by drug addicts with syringes demanding money. Yet, I worked for almost a year without any bad incidents.

When I reflect on that part of my life now, I realise that I was in situations that could have gone badly, encountering drug addicts and kids trying to steal from the shop. Why wasn't I harmed? I did not judge them but made peace with them instead. I talked to them so I could better understand their life and treated them as human beings. My refusal to think of them or treat them as 'bad people, I believe, is what got me through that phase of my working life. We are not born with addiction, after all, but develop it due to individual life circumstances. Despite the dangers, I had wonderful experiences and met fascinating people during my time in Kings Cross.

Understanding what addiction is very important as we are more addicted than ever in human history. By understanding the subtle differences of addiction, obsession, compulsion &

passion we can understand and navigate through the sea of addictions. The influence of society, family, movies, travel, culture, corporations, human consumerism had a big impact on addiction. The inconvenient truth about addiction, is either we normalise it or place a ban and/or try to regulate. It is a taboo with shame and stigma attached on how we perceive others and ourselves going through addiction. Addiction can mean many things to many people, but in general it refers to repeatedly using a substance or engaging in an activity for pleasure, even though doing so causes harm or interferes with our everyday life. Addiction is not limited to Alcohol, Drugs, & Gambling. It extends to other aspects like food habits, social media, sugar, coffee, gaming, religious rituals, exercise, cosmetic, smoking, sex, porn, shopping, pain killers and so on. Addictions are an escapism from whatever we are going through in life. How did we end up as an addicted world, each society, each community, every individual has their own addictions. In one way or another we have our behaviour addictions, an intense desire to repeat some action that is pleasurable or perceived to improve wellbeing.

We are addicted to love, addicted to food, addicted to sex and pornography, addicted to drugs both legal and illegal, addicted to social media, addicted to coffee and tea, addicted to travel, addicted to shopping, addicted to thrill seeking activities, addicted to binge watching, addicted to gaming, addicted to work, addicted to exercise. And the list goes on. Some motivating factors for behavioural addictions include perception of temporary decreased depression and anxiety, to achieve calm or happiness. It can be very difficult to admit to yourself, let alone someone else, that you have a problem. It can even be harder when the problem is not understood and not taken seriously by friends and family. We often get mixed up with the meaning of Addiction, obsession, compulsion and passion.

Addiction is self centered; Passion is generous and not ego driven. Addiction is a thief and takes; Passion is source of truth and gives. Addiction leads into darkness; Passion makes you more alive. Addiction seeks mental escape of the reality; Obsession becomes a ritual routine like excessive hand washing or repetitive counting. Addiction is when someone becomes dependent on a substance or behaviour, compulsion is an intense urge to do something. Compulsion do play a role in the addiction process.

Society is divided and biased when it comes to Addiction. Too much judgmental from moral grounds of what is good and bad. Throughout human history, addiction has gone back and forth between two schools of thought: Is it a choice brought on by the moral values and poor decisions of the afflicted, or is it a legitimate illness that can be addressed through medical and psychiatric approaches? We are addicted to many things & without help and support, we may drift away from life more than we anticipate. Addiction is basically a compulsion to use a certain substance or to behave in a certain way in order to feel good (or sometimes to stop feeling really bad). Addiction falls into two main categories: physical and psychological.

Physical addiction is when your body becomes dependent on a particular substance. It also often means that you've developed a tolerance for the substance, so you must take more of it to continue to feel the effects. If you have a physical addiction, you'll experience strong symptoms of withdrawal when you try to give it up. Examples of physical addiction are drug and alcohol dependence, including cigarettes and prescription painkillers. Psychological addiction is when you're craving for a substance or a behaviour comes from an emotional or psychological desire, rather than from a physical dependence. Your brain is so powerful that it can produce physical symptoms like those of withdrawal, including cravings, irritability and insomnia. Examples of psychological addictions include gambling, gaming, exercise, Internet, shopping, sex and overeating. Several generic signs may indicate that you're addicted to a substance or behaviour. Some examples are, you need to use more of a substance, or to do an activity more often, to get the same effect. You've become reliant on a substance or activity to forget your problems or to relax. You're withdrawing from family and friends. It's causing you problems with school or work. You're stealing or selling stuff to keep doing it such as drugs or gambling. You've been unsuccessful in trying to quit. You feel anxious, angry or depressed. Addiction happens when someone compulsively engages in a behaviour such as drug taking, gambling, drinking or gaming etc. Even when bad side effects kick in and people feel like they're losing control, people who have addictions usually can't stop doing the thing.

I have now been working in the corporate world for over two decades. I began at a large retail brand, then moved to local and global insurance companies. My career so far has been in financial and insurance services, dealing with clients in major industries and across many sectors. Over the years, I have met thousands of people, participated in thousands of meetings, worked through hundreds of different processes, all while trying to fit in and deal with the personalities that come along with corporate life. I have had some great successes, but also failures. Building and maintaining relationships has been paramount in every role I've held, and this has had a considerable impact on who I am today both professionally and personally. I have learned that an understanding of human behaviour is key to achieving my business goals.

My own purpose, and my own values, are different to the typical corporate attitude. What really matters to me is *why* and *how* I can make a difference to the place I work and the people who work with me. I plant a seed, nurture it with water and good sunlight as it grows, then leave just before it starts flowering so that those who come after can enjoy its fruit. This is an approximately three-year cycle and one that I have worked through in each of my corporate roles.

I like to take analogy of corporations and corporate life to a large cargo vessel, in which I am a piece of machinery, working with many other pieces to get the ship safely to its destination. The ship itself is a tiny drop in an enormous ocean, and I am only a small piece within that tiny drop, but the vessel has a purpose and a clear mission. Throughout the journey, we will endure hurricanes, storms, turbulent seas and pirate attacks, but we will also enjoy smooth sailing. It takes time to understand the operations of the whole vessel, and it is not easy to change course, but vessels with advanced machinery are better equipped to face the challenges ahead.

My corporate life has given me wonderful opportunities. It has enabled me to live in different cities and liaise with people from all over the world. Of course, I have had my share of egos to deal with too – power and ego go hand in hand in the corporate hierarchy. Mindset is often determined by which part of the food chain you're working in. Fortunately, I have spent most of my working life at the mid to bottom, in roles that taught me humility and kept me grounded. There, I learned that the corporate world is an ocean, and I can never settle for a pond with boundaries. I must keep striving to satisfy my never-ending hunger to learn more.

Most people wear a mask at work, projecting an image of themselves, a certain way they want to be perceived. While an organisation may start with good intentions – especially in areas like diversity, inclusion, charity and community support initiatives – I fear that most of their employees don't truly believe in these, not in the heart behind their masks. The promotion of diversity, inclusion and social responsibility is commonplace nowadays, and though that has led to new processes, even regulations, in my opinion, most people are slow to accept this change. Rather than address the root cause of our biased human nature, we try to achieve diversity and inclusion through targets. This is surface level, and I have always wondered how we can hope for inclusiveness in corporate world when we remain so separate and divided in society.

Most leaders in the corporate world still follow fifty-year-old business acumen and strategies. Their MBAs and way of thinking are outdated, their definition of success and failure are still related to monetary gain and are not based on social value or doing the right thing. I learned how to survive the corporate world by cultivating patience as deep as the pacific ocean, focussing on process rather than outcome, and treating everyone with respect, regardless of their title, position, or power.

As a Man Thinketh and *The Strangest Secret* are two short works that I have revisited many times. *As a Man Thinketh* is a book of only around thirty pages. *The Strangest Secret* is a spoken word record from 1956, which sold over one million copies and was adapted into print and video. I was introduced to it through the twelve-page essay included in the spoken word format. Both works focus on the power of our thoughts to bring change into our lives. They explore the effect on our character, circumstances, achievements, health and body, and dive into how our mind works and why we may not be able to succeed in life. We can apply and align the message from these books, in the work we do in the corporate world.

These two articles have simple examples and explanations that gave me clarity as I tried to understand my True Self and my actions. They helped me focus on my thoughts, rather than emotions; focus on the process, rather than the outcomes; resist the call of the corporate ladder, and never follow a title or position. With the help of these works, I found my own definition of success and failure, and began to treat my work as a labour of love. What you sow in your mind as thoughts, is what you reap. As Marcus Aurelius said: "A man's life is what his thoughts make of it."

I must be humble in my role in the corporate world, dealing with big egos and strong personalities. This mindset and thought process has helped me find my calm and navigate the troubled waters of the business world. While most workers focus on competence and confidence, I have placed greater emphasis on clarity. The clarity of knowing who I am, what I am doing, where I am going and beyond all that – *why* I am. My purpose. My vision.

As human beings, we react with emotions like fear, anger, sadness, disgust, surprise, and happiness. These fundamental emotions are important for survival: fear warns us about danger, anger directs us to correct perceived wrongs, sadness is a reaction to loss, disgust helps us to expel anything that might be toxic, surprise alerts us to change, and happiness motivates us. There are other emotions like contempt, jealousy, envy, embarrassment, pride, shyness, shame, and guilt. These emotions differ for each person, which can be seen with our facial expressions and body language. By focussing on the thoughts which drive our emotions, we can be more responsive rather than reactive.

The following quotes from the book *As a Man Thinketh* by James Allen

Thought and Character - As a man Thinketh in his heart so is he, not only embraces the whole of a man's being but is so comprehensive as to reach out to every condition and circumstance of his life. A man/woman is literally what he/she thinks, his/her character being the complete sum of all his/her thoughts. Human is made or unmade by self; In the armoury of thought he or she forgets the weapons by which they destroy themselves; also fashions the tools with which they build for themselves mansions of joy, strength and peace. By the right choice and true application of thought, human ascends to the highest level; by the abuse and wrong application of thought, they descend below the level of the beast. Human is the master of thought, the moulded of character, maker shaper of condition, environment, and destiny.

Effect of Thought on Circumstances - Thought and character are one, as character can only manifest and discover itself through environment and circumstance. The outer conditions of a person's life will always be found to be harmoniously related to his/her inner state. This doesn't mean that a human circumstance at any given time is an indication of his/her entire character. But those circumstances are so intimately connected with some vital thought element within self that, for time being, they are indispensable to their development. The outer world of circumstances shapes itself to the inner world of thought, both pleasant and unpleasant external conditions are factors that make for the ultimate good of the individual. Humans don't attract that which they want, but that which they are. Their whims, fancies and ambitions are prevented at every step, but their inmost thoughts and desires are fed with their own food, be it foul or clean.

The divinity that shapes our ends is in ourselves; it is our very self. Only self-restraints humans: Thought and action are in charge of fate - They imprison, they are also the angels of freedom, and they liberate. Not what human wishes and prays for does a man and woman get, but what they justly earn. All the wishes and prayers are only gratified and answered when they harmonise with their thoughts and actions.

Fighting against circumstances - Means that a person is continually revolting against an effect without, while all the time person is nourishing and preserving its cause in his or her heart. That cause may take the form of a conscious vice or an unconscious weakness, but whatever it is, it stubbornly retards the effort of its possessor and calls aloud for remedy. People are anxious to improve their circumstances but are unwilling to improve themselves, they, therefore, remain bound. Good thoughts and actions can never produce bad results; bad thoughts and actions can never produce good results. Suffering is always the effect of wrong thoughts in some direction. It is an indication that the individual is out of harmony with self.

Effect of Thought on Health and the Body - The body is the servant of the mind. Change of diet will not help a person who will not change their thoughts. With pure thoughts, you no longer desire impure food. Clean thoughts make clean habits. Thoughts of malice, envy, disappointment, despondency will rob the body of its health and grace. A sour face doesn't come by chance, it is made by sour thoughts. Those who have lived righteously; age is calm, peaceful, and softly mellowed like the setting sun.

The Thought factor in Achievement - All that a person achieves and all that a person fails to achieve is the direct result of his/her own thoughts. A strong person can't help a weaker unless that weaker is willing to be helped, must become strong of the self. The universe doesn't favour the greedy, dishonest, vicious, although on the mere surface it may sometimes appear to do so. It helps the honest, the magnanimous and virtuous.

All achievements whether in the business, intellectual or spiritual world are the result of directed thought, the only difference lies in the object of attainment. Achievement of whatever kind is the crown of effort, the diadem of thought. By the aid of self-control, resolution, purity, righteousness, and well-directed thought a person ascends; by the aid of animality, indolence, impurity, corruption, and confusion of thought a person descends.

Visions, Ideals and Serenity - To desire is to obtain, to aspire is to achieve. Your vision is the promise of what you shall one day be, your ideal is the prophecy of what you shall at least unveil.

In all human affairs, there are efforts and there are results, and the strength of the effect is the measure of the result. The calmness of mind is the result of long and patient effort in self-control. The calm person having learned how to govern self knows how to adapt self to others and they in turn can learn and rely on the person. The more tranquil a person becomes, the greater is their success, influence, and power of good. Humanity surges with uncontrolled passion is tumultuous with ungoverned grief, is blown about by anxiety and doubt only the wise whose thoughts are controlled and purified, makes the winds and storms of the soul obey him or her.

The following quotes from the article *The Strangest Secret* by Earl Nightingale

This message was first played for a group of salespeople at Earl Nightingale's insurance agency. The most powerful and influential messages ever recorded and continues to transform the lives of everyone who hears and apply in their lives. We live in an era that humanity has looked forward to, dreamed of and worked toward for thousands of years. We live in the richest and best technology era that ever existed on the face of the earth. A land of abundant opportunity for everyone.

However, if you take 100 individuals who start even at the age of 25, they are eager toward life and believe they are going to be successful. But by the time they are 65, only one will be rich, four will be financially independent and others will still be working and or depending on others for life necessities.

Only five out of a hundred make it. Why do so many fail? What happened to the sparkle that was there when they are 25 years old?

Success is the progressive realisation of a worthy ideal. A success is anyone who is realising a worthy predetermined ideal because that's what he/she decided to do deliberately. But the majority end up failures and only one in twenty does that. A reason for so many failures is conformity and people acting like everyone else, without knowing why or where they are going.

Why do so many people work hard and not achieving anything and why others don't seem to work hard yet seem to get everything. The difference is goals. People with goals succeed because they know where they are going, failures believe that their lives are shaped by circumstances, by things that happen to them, by exterior forces

Think of a ship with the complete voyage mapped out and planned. The captain and crew know exactly where the ship is going and how long it will take, it has a definite goal. And 99 times out of 100, it will get there. Now let's take another ship, just like the first, only let's not put a crew on it or a captain at the helm. Let's give it no aiming point, no goal, and no destination. We just start the engines and let it go. I think you will agree that if it gets out of the harbour at all, it will either sink or wind up on some deserted beach, a derelict. It can't go anyplace it has no destination or no guidance. It's the same with human beings.

We become what we think about - This is the strangest secret. Actually, it isn't a secret at all it was first promulgated by the earliest wise people from all cultures, but very few people have learned it or understand it. That's why it's strange and why for some equal reason it virtually remains a secret. A person who is thinking about a concrete and worthwhile goal is going to reach it, because that's what the person is thinking about. Conversely, the person who has no goal, who doesn't know where they are going, whose thoughts must therefore be thoughts of confusion, anxiety, fear, and worry will thereby create a life of frustration, fear, anxiety and worry, and if he/she thinks about nothing becomes nothing.

The human mind doesn't care what we plant: success or failure. But what we plant it must return to us. The human mind is much like a farmer's land. The land gives the farmer a choice. He may plant in that land whatever he chooses. The land doesn't care what is planted. It's up to the farmer to make a decision. The mind like the land will return what you plant, but it doesn't care what you plant. If the farmer plants two seeds - one a seed of corn and the other nightshade a deadly poison, waters and take care of the land, what will happen?

It will return poison in just as wonderful abundance as it will corn. As its written in the bible, "As ye sow, so shall ye reap." The human mind is far more fertile, far more incredible, and mysterious than the land. It does not care what we plant, success or failure. A concrete, worthwhile goal or confusion, misunderstanding, fear, anxiety, and so on. But what we plant it must return. Everything that's worthwhile in life came to us free - our minds, our souls, our bodies, our hopes, our dreams, our ambitions, our intelligence, our love of family and friends. All these priceless possessions are free. But the things that cost us money are cheap and can be replaced at any time. A good person can be completely wiped out and make another fortune. A person can do that several times. But the things we got for nothing; we can never replace.

Every one of us is the sum total of our own thoughts. We must control our thinking. The same rule can lead people to lives of success, wealth, happiness, and all the things they ever dreamed of and that very same law can lead them into the gutter. It's all in how they use it for good or for bad. Whatever you want to achieve, all you got to do is plant that seed in your mind, care for it, work steadily toward your goal and it will become a reality. It works as per the laws of the universe.

Our mind can do any kind of job we assign to it, but we use it for little jobs instead of big ones. Plant your goal in your mind. It's the most important decision you will ever make in your entire life. The moment you decide on a goal to work toward, you are immediately a successful person, you are then in that rare group of people who know where they are going. Out of every hundred people, you belong to the top five. Don't concern yourself too much with how you are going to achieve the goal, leave that completely to a power greater than yourself. All you have to do is know where you are going. The answers will come to you of their own accord, and at the right time.

The most important aspect of our lives, that is finding clarity. How do we find clarity in the world of opinions and expectations. We really need to place greater emphasis on clarity. The clarity of knowing who I am, what I am doing, where I am going and beyond all that – why I am. My purpose. My vision. We all have different roles and responsibilities in life, each role comes with its own expectations and pressure. As a husband, wife, lover, father, mother, brother, sister, friend, son, daughter, work and so on. As human beings in our different roles, we react with emotions like fear, anger, sadness, disgust, surprise, and happiness. These fundamental emotions are important for survival: fear warns us about danger, anger directs us to correct perceived wrongs, sadness is a reaction to loss, disgust helps us to expel anything that might be toxic, surprise alerts us to change, and happiness motivates us. There are other emotions like contempt, jealousy, envy, embarrassment, pride, shyness, shame, and guilt. These emotions differ for each person, which can be seen with our facial expressions and body language. By focusing on the thoughts which drive our emotions, we can be more responsive rather than reactive.

We become what we think about, what we manifest. The vast difference between success and failure is in their goals and manifestation. People with goals succeed because they know where they are going, failures believe that their lives are shaped by circumstances, by things that happen to them, by exterior forces. Everything has will in everything we do. It is a consciousness of willingness and of being that may differ in degree from that of humans, but not in substance. We are equipped with brain and memories and means of recording emotions and thoughts, and yet we are unconscious major part of a single day's living. The creation is conscious of your unconsciousness and that of every creature in the universe. Be mindful of how you breathe, and how you speak and what you wish, think, and do. For your Will is hid in every breath, every word, every wish, thought and deed. And what is hid from you is always manifest to the existence/universe

Till we grow conscious of all things we cannot be conscious of others in us, nor us in them. Till we are conscious of all things in us, we cannot know the mysteries of the universe. All that a person achieves and all that a person fails to achieve is the direct result of his/ her own thoughts. The universe doesn't favour the greedy, dishonest, vicious, although on the mere surface it may appear to do so. It helps the honest, the magnanimous and virtuous.

We don't need to leave our so-called 'normal' life and go to the Himalayas or become a hermit, to attain clarity, peace and pleasantness. Humans don't attract that which they want, but that which they are.

CHAPTER THREE

From Separation to Union

A reflection on knowledge and teachings
by authors since 2015

Just over twelve years ago, I separated from my previous partner. When I look back at the relationship now, I realise that many of the reasons for our breakup were due to my own selfishness. After my mother's passing, and my marriage in India, came the discussion about kids. As the eldest son in the family, I was under considerable pressure to have children. However, we were unable to conceive naturally and began IVF (In vitro fertilization is a process of fertilization where an egg is combined with sperm in vitro, outside the living body) in 2007.

I was very naïve about the process of IVF and the toll it would take on us. Every cycle lasts four to six weeks. Each time, my partner endured two weeks of daily injections and all the side effects that come along with that, such as abdominal pain and bruising, nausea, bloating, fatigue, mood swings and anxiety. The ups and downs of investing so heavily in the process, giving it her all, only to have her hopes dashed when a cycle did not end with pregnancy, created emotional stress that can't be underestimated. It grew into a fruitless, expensive odyssey, but we persevered, clinging to the hope that surely the next cycle would be successful.

At first, I embraced the procedure and tried to remain supportive, but as the months dragged on with no results, it began to wear on me too. Altogether we did six cycles but had no luck. At one point we discussed the possibility of adopting instead, but my partner was determined to keep trying. To be honest, the process was far more demanding on her than it was on me. I felt helpless and followed the process deep inside knowing it is distancing our relationship.

We were happily surprised when the seventh cycle resulted in a pregnancy, but the doctors warned us to be vigilant. The developing embryo's heartbeat was not where it should be. For two weeks, we went in for a daily check-up. For two weeks, it felt like we were holding our breath. Those were the longest two weeks of my life, and despite everything my partner went through, everything we did together, they ended in miscarriage and heartbreak. Our tiny struggling embryo did not survive.

At this point, to stop us both from being overwhelmed by our grief, I decided we needed a holiday in India. This, I hoped, would get our minds off IVF. Travelling in a minibus with my family, my ex-partner, and her mother, across four South Indian states were surely as far as we could get from doctors and injections and cycles. We were inspired by the *Reader's Digest Illustrated Guide to India* but allowed the journey to be spontaneous – made no plans and booked nothing ahead, just let the road take us where we needed to be.

Our road trip began in Tirupati (a town close to where my father was born), in the state of Andhra Pradesh. From there, we headed towards the state of Karnataka. I can still see the city of Bangalore's magical botanic gardens clearly in my mind, as well as the Ulsoor lake and Tipu Sultan's (who ruled from the late 18th Century) summer palace. At Mysore we took a family photo in front of the Amba Villas palace at night, as thousands of lights enlivened the exterior, making it shimmer with gold. We stopped at Hampi, a city carved in stone on the banks of the river Tungabhadra, and a UNESCO world heritage site. In the 1500s – the 'golden age' of South India – this was the capital of the South

Indian rulers, where they traded in pearls and precious stones in street markets. I remember it as a beautiful, peaceful place, where we saw elephant stables, the Queen's bathhouse with its natural air conditioning, and the erotic carvings at the temple to Lord Shiva. Another temple we visited in Hampi had small, hollow columns that play music when lightly tapped. From there, we travelled through Kerala, a state full of beautiful natural scenery, and spent time in Kochi (Cochin city). I can still taste the tea I drank at Ooty, a spot in the Nilgiri (blue) hills famous for its plantations and cooler climate. At Pondicherry, where French is still spoken, we ate baguettes for breakfast. In the state of Tamil Nadu, we visited Mahabalipuram, the site of a group of UNESCO world heritage listed monuments built by the Pallava dynasty in the 7th and 8th Centuries. And this was only the beginning.

We covered around 3000 km in two weeks, visited many heritage-listed sites during our trip, met many locals and experienced the unconditional love and affection that life offers. One of my strongest memories is a photo I took of my ex-partner in a field of sunflowers that stretched as far as the eye could see. Experiencing nature, people, history, wildlife and food in this way is precious. They say that the longest distance you travel in life is from your head to your heart. This trip was one of those journeys you feel in your heart, and it will always be a part of me. When we returned to Sydney, the next IVF cycle was successful, and my daughter was born in June 2009.

Even as this was happening, I was still drifting away from my ex-partner. Sometimes it felt like I was searching for ways to create more distance between us. One of these was financial. After witnessing my mother's death from cancer, and my father's illness and recovery, I wanted to start a small clinic to facilitate earlier diagnoses, near a village where my family owns small land. To make this work, I entered a business venture with my brother and some friends. We raised a significant amount of money, and I poured myself into the work, spending far more time and energy on it than on my relationship... only to learn it had all been a scam.

I lost every penny I invested in the business, sending us almost bankrupt. I made hundreds of phone calls and sent hundreds of emails trying to get answers. This became a very difficult time for me, as I struggled under the emotional and financial burden of this betrayal. Initially, I tried to make people accountable for misleading me, but when I realised this was going nowhere – and that it was not good for my mental health either – I decided not to waste any more of my time or energy dwelling on what was lost.

Twelve months later, in April 2011, my partner and I decided to separate. In all honesty, my heart simply wasn't in the relationship anymore. I was taking it for granted, refusing to prioritize what I already had. It took nearly two years for my family to accept the breakdown of my marriage. To them, divorce simply wasn't an option, so they refused to believe it. Once they finally accepted the truth, they immediately brought me new proposals of arranged marriage. But I stuck to my guns and was very firm with them – I would not under any circumstances, entertain the idea of an arranged marriage.

Despite the circumstances of our breakup, I was at peace with my choices and my actions. I knew that I was the problem and the decision we had made was for the good of my daughter and ex-partner. Some nights, in the loneliness and emptiness, my thoughts began to spiral towards darkness. But I was already strong enough to recognise what was happening, differentiate and overcome those thoughts. I decided to let everything go and restart my life. I quit my well-paid job (even though my colleagues and friends thought it was a stupid thing to do – and told me so!) and moved to Europe. I lived and worked there for a year and a half.

My daughter was two years old when we divorced, and for a long time, I was not able to see her. While others tried to convince me to follow up on my legal right to visitation, I knew that wasn't the right step. Instead, I believed that if I could heal our relationship and gain her trust, I would be able to see her through love, not force. My time in Europe ended in 2013, and

I headed back to Sydney to see her. I don't think she recognised me at first and didn't even want to come close to me, but she was only four years old. While I knew better than to take it personally, my mind was still trying to control me with emotion – there were tears in my eyes, I felt heavy in the head and lonely as a child, lost in a busy shopping centre, searching for my mother. After a short walk-in a nearby garden, my heart was able to take back control over my mind and give me the clarity I needed: that this was temporary, and my emotional reaction to the situation was temporary too, but what is permanent, what is never changing, is always with us in our hearts.

After a short time in Sydney, I moved to Melbourne and started a new job in June 2013. It was a bit of a step backwards for me, but I didn't care. For the four months before I moved to Melbourne, I did it tough. I had little money for myself and lived in a share house. I recall days when I didn't have enough money for food, so I found hotels that offered free meals to gamblers and would drop a dollar into the machines and pretend to be playing. I met the liveliest characters in these venues, and regret none of my time there. These moments taught me that when you have basic needs like food, shelter, health and clothing, the rest is just a bonus.

It helped me to think of all the events in my life like passing clouds – some are nice to watch and experience and others cause lightning, thunder, and chaos. But they all pass. I thought this way to shake off any feelings of victimhood on my part.

When I moved to Melbourne, I took a 40% cut to my salary, compared to my previous job. But I needed the stability of a regular income to get back on track financially and support my daughter. To get to Melbourne in the first place, I borrowed money from a friend, and for a month and a half I lived in backpacker accommodation. I shared a four-bunkbed room and enjoyed the opportunity to meet friendly young people from all over the world. I'm pretty sure I was the only person to turn up to breakfast in a tie and a suit! Without money for lunch or dinner, I relied on the free coffee, biscuits and snacks they provided at work.

When I look back at this time in Melbourne, I do so with joy. In every moment I felt truly alive, knowing that what was coming next would be better and better. It was rich with opportunity. After receiving my first month's salary, I found a place to rent and started a stable life in Melbourne. During this time, I visited Sydney often and began a routine where I could see my daughter almost every second month. Slowly, the love and trust between us grew. In 2016, my work presented me with an opportunity to move back to Sydney, and since then my time with my daughter has increased, from bi-monthly, to monthly, to every second week, and now weekly. Our bond is strong because I allowed our relationship to develop naturally.

It is difficult to find the words to express the depth of the connection I feel with my daughter. Heightened by our time apart, it feels like every moment we spend together is precious, no matter what we do. I will never take any of it for granted. She is more than a fifteen-year-old child to me; she is an individual with her own personality – one I am conscious not to influence too much. I am simply here to support her in her own being. Every week, I go to her soccer games. We enjoy regular lunches and love watching movies together. Our discussions are pure, without bias, and a lot more rewarding than those I have with most adults! As she enters her teenage years and then her adult life, I know she will want and need more time to herself, so I make the most of these childhood years. She is developing her wings, and soon she will be ready to fly away and explore the world on her own terms.

One of the regular activities I do with my daughter is to visit my local library. While I was there with her, just browsing one day, I came across three books: *Lagom*, *Hygge* and *Ikigai*. I always wondered why Japan and the Nordic countries rank among the top ten happiest nations in the world, and these three books have helped me to understand that. They gave me clarity on important elements of Japanese and Nordic culture that flow as an undercurrent to their modern societies and contribute to their 'happiness ranking'. According to the world happiness report, five Nordic countries Finland, Denmark, Norway, Sweden and Iceland have all been in the top ten happiest nations in the world. Nordic citizens experience a high sense of autonomy and freedom, as well as high levels of social trust towards each other, which play an important role in determining life satisfaction. Autonomy and the freedom to make life choices are known to be connected to subjective wellbeing. The extent to which a country is able to provide individuals a sense of agency, freedom, and autonomy plays a significant role in explaining citizen happiness. Trust in other people and social cohesion has also been linked to citizen happiness. As a community, your basic needs are met, so you are not living in constant fear of going broke. They trust one another, foster communities, and feel gratitude. They make time to spend together, everyone does it a little differently. Danes do *Hygge*, comfortable indulgences to bond together. Finns have their saunas, a sacred tradition dating back thousands of years with rules and customs. Swedes famously have *fika*, which translates to coffee, also means a culturally mandatory social hour, that everyone takes time around the same time. Coffee breaks are mandatory, everything drops, not to be on their phone, but to converse with each other and make most of the fika time to bond. Calling out friends if they are picking up unhealthy habits and Norwegians prefer that people strive not to stand out from the group too much, so being humble and not brag too much about achievements keeps everyone grounded. One's gratitude and being appreciative of life is crucial to maintaining happiness.

Lagom is the Swedish philosophy of 'moderation in everything' aims to balance in every area and juncture of everyday life. Hygge is the Danish focus on presence and togetherness. Ikigai is the Japanese understanding of the purpose of life. I have also included here a summary of 'The Yogi Code', another text which focuses on bringing everything we learn into the practice of daily life, and the importance of asking ourselves, 'what do I really want?'

Lagom, the Swedish secret of living well and balanced living. The word translates to in moderation, in balance, just enough, ideal and suitable, perfect and simple. Not too much, not too little, the right amount is the best and enough is as good as a feast. There is virtue in moderation. Where there is modesty there is a virtue. Living with less and being happy. The concept is based on opposition to any excess and find balance as a true goal. Knowing how to stay positive in every situation, able to learn from every experience, aspiring to live fairly and in harmony with the world. Lagom lifestyle is based on sustainability, energy saving and the use of materials that respect the environment, to reuse and give new life to used objects. A simple but functional house, with harmony, moderation, utility and versatility. The well-known furniture brand Ikea has dedicated to Lagom their entire line of furniture, characterised by simplicity, cleanliness, practicality and convenience.

Food - Eat sustainably, ethically and locally. The principle of simplicity applies in the kitchen, based on a concept of sustainability and the use of genuine ingredients. Mindful of the consumption of meat and not to buy food that results from practices of unsustainable and harmful to environment. Our actions are in the best interests of the greater good of social consciousness. Breakfast less is more. Coffee breaks are to give our minds rest and balance our thoughts and emotions. Reconnect with ourselves.

Well-being - Best way to take care of loved ones is to love and take care of ourselves first. Better an honest No than an insincere Yes. Find time for both exercise and rest, both activities that purify the mind and help to deal with everyday life in a positive spirit. Finding simple activity and indulging in little joys to ourselves to get away from the anxieties or worries of work or family.

Beauty - Appreciate your natural beauty without hiding it under layers of make-up. The virtue of minimalism is that it psychologically frees us from unnecessary tasks and responsibilities that weigh us down. In addition to this freedom, it also lets us see our own tastes and preferences more clearly against a clutter free backdrop. Anything outside practical or emotional can be removed.

In business, Lagom chooses logic over emotion. Practicality over vision, action over-promise. Our actions and the words we speak to be binding long before we physically sign any contracts. We are all fundamentally equal and should be treated that way, regardless of our social titles or cultural standing. One who proves too much proves nothing. No letters are good letters. Empty barrels rattle the most. Negotiate from a place of empathy for both sides.

Finance - Anything falls outside functional and or sentimental value can be considered excess or useless. Don't judge all you see, don't believe all you hear, don't do all you can, don't say all you know, don't eat all you have, let no one know what you have in your heart or in your wallet.

Better be silent than speak ill, overpraise is a burden. Listen more and speak less. What we feel we want maybe a thin veil over what we really need and so fully attending to those basal needs may very well satisfy our wants and push us closer to contentment. Lagom is a luxury of thought that thrives against a backdrop where our basic needs are adequately met. It sharpens our curiosity and consciousness what can I do to feel content and balanced today.

Hygge, a Danish art of living well is a quality of presence and an experience of togetherness. Creating a warm atmosphere and enjoying good things in life with good people. Taking time away from the daily rush to be together with people you care about or even by yourself to relax and enjoy life's small pleasures. Hygge is often about informal time together with family and close friends without an agenda. The concept is rooted in comfort, togetherness and well-being. Celebrating the small joys of life, or maybe discuss deeper topics, taking an opportunity to unwind and take things slow. A general sense of comfort, charm, simplicity and community, like the German idea of *gemütlichkeit*, the Dutch term *gezelligheid* and the Swedish word *mys*.

German word Gemütlichkeit convey the idea of a state or feeling warmth, friendliness and good cheer coming from cosiness, peace of mind, sense of belonging, contentment and well-being springing from social acceptance.

Dutch word Gezelligheid convey as cosiness, fun, relaxed situation often when time spent with loved ones, family and friends, a general togetherness that gives people a warm feeling. Individuals well being that typically shares with others, involves a positive atmosphere, flow or vibe.

Swedish word Mys or Mysa translates to cosiness, involves being relaxed, taking time out from stress, spending time with friends, and being in the moment, enjoying it with all your senses. Fika, Lagom and Mys are all Swedish concepts of well being and living a happy simple life.

Belonging to the moment - Hygge entails a commitment to the present moment and a readiness to set distractions aside. Hygge isn't about a life without technology, but it asks us to balance our commitments and remember the value of human interaction, conversation and physical intimacy. Cooking, eating and cleaning up together is very hygge. Playing games together is a great way to be present. Sharing a movie with friends and family can be very hygge. The best number of people for hygge activities is less than five.

Shelter - A basic sense of security. Spaces are created for solitude and participation, privacy and sociability, stillness and sound. Nature is encouraged to embrace a home. Shelter is about the people and things that bring peace. Harmony at home can't be purchased or bought, it requires everyone's presence and togetherness. *Comfort* - Consciously practised in many everyday lives, something commonplace but rarely taken for granted. It's associated with the comfort of routine and everyday rituals. The idea of comfort is about letting yourself relax. You are not trying to impress anyone. You should keep in mind is your comfort should not come at the expense of another person's comfort. *Wellbeing* - A deep rapport with ourselves and the world around us. Contentment by having a strong societal conscience. Balance in all areas of life, naturally seeking equilibrium through moderation and compromise. *Simplicity* - As simple as a candle. It is both an inner and outer condition of simplicity, clarity of presence and intentions. *Observance* - Any moment is an opportunity to savour a feeling of belonging togetherness.

Taking time to appreciate the good things in your life is hygge. Gratitude and being grateful for all the simple things in life. Making space for what is important in life. I read a beautiful story about the 'Rocks, Pebbles and Sand', reminds me of finding joy in life depends on how much space you create within you for what matters most and life priorities.

A philosophy professor who was giving a lecture had a big glass jar, a pile of rocks, a bag of small pebbles & a tub of sand. He started off by filling up the jar with the big rocks and when they reached the rim of the jar, he held it up to the students and asked them if the jar was full.

They all agreed, there was no more room for the rocks, it was full.

He then picked up the bag of small pebbles and poured in jar. He shook the jar so that the pebbles filled the space around the big rocks. "Is the jar full now?" he asked. The group of students all looked at each other and agreed that the jar was now completely full.

The professor then picked up the tub of sand. He poured the sand in between the pebbles and the rocks and once again he held up the jar to his class and asked if it was full. Once again, the students agreed that the jar was full.

The professor went on to explain that the jar of rocks, pebbles, sand represents everything that is in one's life.

The jar represents your life. The rocks represent the most important things that have real value, which is your health, family, partner & wellbeing. The pebbles represent the things in your life that matter, but that you could live without, such as your job, house, hobbies and friendships, but they are not critical for you to have a meaningful life. These things often come and go and are not permanent. The sand represents everything else, the small stuff, such as watching television or browsing social media sites, material things. These things don't mean much to your life as a whole and are likely done to get small tasks accomplished or even to pass time.

The metaphor here is, if you start with filling sand into the jar, you will not have room for rocks or pebbles. If you spend all your time on the small and insignificant things, you will run out of room for the things that are important.

Make room for what's important. Take care of the rocks first – the things that really matter and are critical to your long-term wellbeing, joy & peace. Prioritize the big rocks of life by practicing self-care, spending quality time with people you love, and the rest is just pebbles and sand, they will always find some space.

Ikigai is the Japanese secret to a long and happy life. It is a concept that encourages people to discover what truly matters to them and to live a life filled with purpose and joy. Iki means to live, and Gai means reason. A reason to live. A reason to get up in the morning.

Ikigai is a lifestyle that strives to balance the spiritual with the practical. One of the biggest mistakes people make in life is believing that money leads to happiness and fulfilment. First you need to find what you are most passionate about and find a medium through which you can express that passion. In doing so, the money is one of the outcomes. Ikigai is a state of well being that comes from devotion to activities one enjoys, which brings a sense of fulfilment and contentment. It is a similar concept to the ancient Greek sense *hedonia* and *eudaimonia*, which is a positive and divine state of being that humanity can strive towards simple happiness. A happiness coming from doing what feels good, what feels right, from the pursuit of authenticity, meaning, virtue and growth.

The journey of Ikigai is an intersection of passion, talent, and contribution to others, which requires time, self-reflection and effort. A philosophical modern perspective of Ikigai holds a central position of four areas of life. What you love, what you are good at, what the world needs, what you get paid for. At the intersection of what you love and what you are good at is your *passion*. At the intersection of what you love and what the world needs is your *mission*. At the intersection of what the world needs and what you get paid for is your *occupation*. At the intersection of what you are good at and what you can get paid for is your *profession*. The Ikigai is a sweet spot of something you are passionate about, that you are so good at, that the world needs, and for which someone will pay you. The zen Buddhist mindset of Ikigai emphasises on being active, being in the moment, taking joy in the small things in life and finding a state of flow in one's life.

The five pillars of Ikigai are starting small, releasing yourself, harmony and sustainability, joy of little things, being in the here and now. Ask yourself, your most sentimental values and the small things that give you pleasure. In order to practice mindfulness, it is important to attend to the here and now, without rushing to make judgements.

Eihei-Ji Temple in Japan translates to temple of eternal peace. It is a monastery and there is no merit system. You are treated like any other regular disciple; you become an anonymous being, almost invisible; individuality loses any sense of relevance. They have succeeded in releasing themselves. Relieving ourselves of the burden of the self, we can open to the infinite universe of sensory pleasures a significant attribute of consciousness.

Flow and creativity (state of flow) - People are so involved in an activity that nothing else seems to matter. You find pleasure in work. You work because working itself gives you immense pleasure. Wages are a bonus. Work becomes an end in itself, rather than something to be endured as a means of achieving something. You are not the master, work is the master and inflow, you can identify yourself with your work in a joyous, symbiotic way.

Ichigo Ichie (one time one encounter) - Comes from a tea ceremony tradition. The appreciation of short encounters with people, things, or events in life. Take notice of small details of life, nothing is repeated.

Five pillars of Ikigai are embodied in a tea ceremony. *Starting small* - The master carefully prepares the room with utmost attention to detail. *Releasing oneself* - The spirit of humility is the hallmark of the tea master and guests. *Harmony and sustainability* - Many wares used to resonate with each other. *The joy of little things* - Utmost goal of a tea ceremony is to be relaxed, to take pleasure in the sensory details within the tearoom. *Being in the here and now* - To be in a state of mindfulness.

Once you achieve a state of blissful connection and concentration, an audience is not necessary. There are delays between actions and rewards.

Ise grand shrine, Japan's most sacred shrine dates back to almost 2000 years old, and the most fascinating fact about the shrine is that every 20 years rebuilding of the shrine in alternative sites of the inner and outer shrine of Ise as well as the Uji bridge happens. This is the belief of rebirth and renewal. The shrine is a great example of sustainability, and sustainability is an art of life. An individual is like a forest, yet connected and dependent on others for growth. The Ise Grand Shrine located in Ise, Mie Prefecture of Japan, is a Shinto shrine dedicated to the sun goddess Amaterasu. Followers of Shintoism worship their ancestors and regard them as the guardians of the family. They focus on the relationship between plants, animals, people, the elements and the yearly cycles of growth, death and rebirth. The architectural style of the Ise shrine is known as shinmei-zukuri, characterized by extreme simplicity and antiquity; its basic principles date back to 250–538 C.E. To mark the importance of the circle of life the shrine buildings at Naiku and Geku, as well as the Uji Bridge, are rebuilt every 20 years as a part of the Shinto belief of the death and renewal of nature and the impermanence of all things and as a way of passing building techniques from one generation to the next. Every 20 years the shrine is demolished and then rebuilt, to the same dimensions but on an alternate site within the precinct. The process involves around 30 different rituals and ceremonies. To date, it has been rebuilt 62 times, most recently in 2013 and scheduled for rebuilding in 2033.

Ikigai is an adaptation to the environment, no matter what the nature of that environment might be. Ikigai and happiness come from the acceptance of the self, no matter what kind of unique features one might happen to be born with.

In many ways, Japanese culture is rich, and we can apply and practice their concepts for self-improvement and a balanced life.

Omoiyari means caring and showing sincere consideration for others. Practicing omoiyari is said to help build compassion and empathy toward others. Embedded compassion in your life & work.

Ikigai a state of well-being induced by devotion to enjoyable activities, which leads to a sense of fulfillment. It is said that in Japan, people who have a purpose in life live longer. Your ikigai is what gets you up every morning and keeps you going. Live with purpose and passion.

Wabi-sabi is a concept that encourages us to embrace our imperfections and accept the natural cycle of life. Be grateful, see beauty in imperfection, and strive for excellence, not perfection.

Mottainai means respecting the resources we have, not wasting them, and using them with a sense of gratitude. Uniqlo uses "Mottainai: Old Clothes, New Life" to achieve zero waste. Embrace essentialism and live sustainably.

Shin-Gi-Tai translates as "mind, technique, and body." Mind, technique, and body are the three elements for maximum performance used in martial arts. A healthy body and a sound mind are the foundation for developing and refining any skills. keep a healthy body and a sound mind. They are the path to mastery.

Shu-Ha-Ri translates as "follow, breakaway, and transcend." It is a way of thinking about how to learn and master a technique. Learn the basics. Imitate, then innovate. There are 3 stages to acquiring knowledge:

Shu: learn the basics by following the teaching of one master. Imitating the work of great masters also falls in this stage.

Ha: start experimenting, learn from masters, and integrate the learning into the practice.

Ri: This stage focuses on innovation and adapting the learning to different situations.

Kaizen is a method of continuous improvement based on the theory that small, ongoing positive changes can be significant. Kaizen reminds us to let go of assumptions and perfectionism. It teaches us to take an iterative, progressive approach to change. Embrace change and strive for small and continuous improvements.

Mono no aware is a concept of having empathy towards things and their inevitable passing. This concept reminds us that nothing in life is permanent. We should willingly and gracefully let go of our attachments to transient things. Detach from material things, outcomes, and old beliefs.

Omotenashi is a concept about offering the best service without expecting a reward. It's an important part of Japanese culture and deeply rooted in how Japanese society functions. Give without expecting a reward.

Ho-Ren-So translates as "report, inform, and consult." The concept forms the basis of all communication, collaboration, and healthy information sharing in a Japanese organization. It focuses on the roots of the communication line, streamlining the flow of information, and preventing issues from happening again. The Japanese argument is that the Ho-Ren-So, through collaboration and communication, strengthens subordinate employee relationships and provides a platform for the subordinate to learn from their superior. It is good practice to encourage everyone to report issues and problems immediately. Even if a solution is not found, the cost of a problem that is not reported can be high. Communicate. Report problems even if you don't have an answer.

I love Japanese Zen stories which taught me lot about life. A story about cup of tea teaches us about being open to learning.

Nan-In, a Japanese master during the Meiji era, (1868–1912), received a university professor who came to inquire about Zen. The professor heard that the master knows everything about life and wanted to test him. After waiting for a long time feeling impatient, finally the master appeared and served tea. He poured his visitor's cup full, and then kept on pouring.

The professor watched the overflow until he no longer could restrain himself. "It's overfull. No more will go in!"

"Like this cup," Nan-in said, "you are full of your own opinions and speculations. How can I show you Zen unless you first empty your cup?"

The Zen master was trying to tell the professor that he couldn't teach the art of Zen to a university professor full of book knowledge. Universities are about accumulating knowledge, which is intellectual, whereas Zen is about throwing it away which is intelligence. Having a Zen mind will enable you to learn anything faster. Through Zen, you get in touch with your intuition.

In the beginner's mind there are many possibilities; in the expert's mind there are few.

According to the yogi code, we have seven areas to focus.
Routine - Create daily routines to enhance your vitality, focus and

power. *Practice* - Adapt daily practices that create calm, clarity, and a good psychological foundation. *Self-study* - Learn methods for understanding your true nature and expand your current potential. *Intention* - Unveil and understand your every intention in practical ways. *Purpose* - Discover how to reveal and live for a purpose. *Service* - Empower yourself through an attitude of service to others. *Love* - Tap into the power of the universe by unfolding the force of nature which is love.

A routine is not to limit you, but to help you live with specific intentions and to support your goals. Respect the importance of setting healthy habits, balance the boundaries of necessities and lower the need for extras. Sadhana is a practice throughout our lifetime. Pure sadhana makes you feel universal and not just worldly.

In silence there is clarity, in noise there is confusion. In stillness there is calm, in excess motion there is excess nervous energy. Peace, purpose, and even-mindedness can take the state of mind from thinking to being. This is an even greater place to be than happiness; as happiness also has an extreme opposite, which is sadness.

The key to who you are is discovering your higher self by coming out of fake self and ego self. Higher Self is the witness, soul, intuition, super consciousness and divine. It is the energy of the universe within us. Path of self-surrender and self-observation. To reach a higher state of consciousness speak less, read more and practice everything you learn.

Our intentions come from the purest level driven by our heart's desire (selfless) and not our mind's desire (individual ego). Our intentions for why we do something affect our attitude and behaviour towards it. The more extreme events and life experiences we have been through, the deeper and more concrete many of our intentions become. First, know where your intentions are coming from. Second, do you have a deep inner intention. Third, is your intention in line with your true inner character and nature.

Every action has an intention even if you don't know it at the time, there is always a reason for everything. Absolutely everything that happens in your life, the world and the universe has a purpose and reason. Our purpose as soul travellers is liberation. Liberation from the physical body and liberation from the material plane. Liberation comes once we achieve our life purpose and fulfil dharma (right way of living and behaviour) during this lifespan. So, we have one purpose to live for and one to die for.

Practice peacefulness, practice creative control (sexual energy) and avoid burdensome excesses, the concept of not taking or consuming more than we need. Service is different from helping, helping another is more ego-mind concept than actual service. We guide others to help themselves through changes they have decided to make. True service is an attitude that we bring into our actions and not just the action itself.

Climate change and environmental challenges - We are polluting the earth at a rapid pace, but the earth doesn't need our help. What we need is not to help the planet, but to be of service to it by curbing our individual and collective toxic lifestyles of excessive consumption and using more than we need.

Spirituality and acting out of consciousness is not an intellectual process. Being of true service is to act out of our hearts spirit in a selfless way and put the other person first no matter who they are and what they have done. Electricity is current, and a current is an energy. Love is just a current of energy. To love without condition is to love purely. Love is not a feeling but a state of being.

What do you really want? Need to answer this before moving forward. To find answer to this, you need to take the longest journey you will ever make in your life, that is from your head to the heart. The Source we are all seeking is in our heart, where we all meet as one and don't judge. Yet our minds and heads are limiting us. We are giving more preference to our heads rather than understanding the magic of our hearts. Intellect is crucial for your survival. But intellect is becoming a barrier because you keep it constantly dipped in the accumulative part of the mind which is your memory. Most of us are still stuck with the Intellect and Memory, instead of focusing on Awareness, which is the window to our heart. Human Mind is manufacturing a million ways to suffer. Once you are no longer identified with your mind, you are free to experience life beyond limitations. Being aware means, you have become a witness to your own intellect, who has transcended intellect, discriminatory and logical dimensions of life.

The Mind turned inwards is the self, turned outwards it becomes the ego and all the world. The self exists without the mind, never the mind without the self.

Heart is the core of one's being, the centre without which there is nothing whatever. The heart is from which thoughts arise, on which they subsist and where they are resolved. The thoughts are the content of the mind, and they shape the universe. The heart is the centre of all. The consciousness which is the real existence, and which doesn't go out to know things other than self alone is the heart. The universe is just a play of five elements water, fire, earth, air and ether. Once you are in touch with your awareness which is nothing but your heart, you don't have to try to accomplish anything. The best possible thing that can happen to you will happen. Once you distance yourself from the compulsiveness of your own genetic and karmic information, life becomes unburdened, flexible, incredibly effortless. Pure consciousness of being is the heart. From heart arises 'I Am' ness as the primary point of one's experience. You can get a bed made of pure gold, but not a peaceful or pleasant sleep. Freedom means being able to reject the leadership of the majority and not follow popularity. The heart that gives, gathers. Stillness is the ruler of movement. The world is a spiritual vessel and cannot be controlled. Trying to control the world, you won't succeed. Those who control, fail. Those who grasp, lose. Vast is the difference between holding and being held. You hold only what you love, what you hate holds you. Avoid being held.

Whoever cannot find a temple in their heart, the same can never find their heart in any temple. The most beautiful moments in your life, are the moments when you are not thinking about anything. When the room is dark, a lamp is necessary to illuminate and eyes to see the objects. But when the sun has risen there is no need for a lamp to see the objects. To see the sun no lamp is necessary, it is enough that you turn your eyes towards the self-luminous sun. Similarly, with the mind, to see the objects, the reflected light of the mind is necessary. To see the heart, it is enough that the mind is turned towards it. Then the mind loses itself and the heart shines forth. I gained a better understanding of how thought and emotion create a conflict between our head and heart. Thought has a certain clarity, whereas with emotion it takes time. The distinction between 'me' and 'my mind' is the first step to freedom. Don't be scared by the fears in your mind, be led by the heart. It is only with the heart that one can see rightly, which is invisible to the eyes of the mind. Understanding how our mind functions enable us to better handle stress and anxiety, through an awareness of Self, connecting with our Heart. Awareness is not something that we do, awareness is what we are, our heart. Once we are in touch with our awareness, we don't have to try to accomplish anything. The best possible thing that can happen to us, will happen. When heart speaks, head simply follows without any objections. We all experience this when we are falling in love with someone. We simply fall in love; nothing stops us and we are ready to climb seven mountains and swim seven seas to reach the love. The one within you who can observe your own thoughts is your heart. Trust your heart, follow your heart, listen to your hearts inner voice, don't care about what others think or try to meet society expectations.

Food and energy, the most important aspects of our wellbeing. Food represents matter & energy is our spirit. Body is the accumulation of food; Mind is the accumulation of ideas, and our spirit is our energy. The sole aim of every individual life energy is to touch the infinite, the very core of our making. Life energies are always longing to break the boundaries set by your physical (body) and mental (mind) structures. The content of physical and mental bodies has been gathered from outside. They belong to you, but they are not you. Manage body and mind consciously, then your experience of life is your making. All you need to do is create a distance between you and everything that you have accumulated from outside. We often complicate the word energy by trying to define it in scientific or spiritual terms. All we need to understand energy is to get quiet and feel into ourselves or our surroundings. Energy can neither be created nor destroyed but can be channelled. People who practice meditation, yoga, and/or certain spiritual religious activities are nothing but the experiences of energy within us. Another example most people experience is when you go to your favourite music concert, watching your favourite movie star on first day first show or favourite sports game at a big stadium, you will feel the energy both within and from others. Thats why those moments stay with us as the best moments in our life. The energy in us is in free flow, pure joy and happiness. On the other hand, A closed mind is an energy block, when our belief system is fixed, we are blocked. When we lack faith in the process or in ourselves, our energy is blocked. An example of how energy has an impact

Take a young girl, every night when the father comes home, she runs to him and jumps into his arms. Each time she does this, imagine her father pushes away knowingly or unknowingly. The child begins to contract and restrict her excitement and the physical impulse to run towards him. She also begins to make up a story to make sense of her experience, which might be rejection, abandonment and lack of love. The little girl in her adult life, will struggle to express her feelings, and will experience the feeling of physically distant in relationships. Her energy life force is blocked, this is the free energy of the child following the natural impulse to run and jump into the arms of life. As you begin to become more conscious of your actions and energy, pieces of the life puzzle will come together.

Your energy and thoughts are not just powerful, they are the key to your life. The law of energy says that everyone has within them the power to change the conditions of their lives. Sadly, only a small percentage of humanity ever utilises this power. Your joy, misery, love, agony, bliss lie in your energy. There is a way out, and the way out is by understanding your energy. Thoughts are forms of energy, become aware of your thinking. Notice your first thought of the day. Close your eyes and feel your deep breathe and the flow at times during the day. Notice how you are moving your body. Observe your voice and words. Observe your energy and body, both within yourself and in others. You will start to see miracles and magical experience. Be an observer of your own thoughts, actions, breathing, voice, words, body movements, you will start to notice miracles happening every day. Try to watch a sunrise and sunset every day, or spend time in nature, you will start to notice the life energy within you and around you.

'Inner Engineering' is another book which helped me gain clarity on many aspects of my life. Sadhguru's explanations are simple but deep. He reflects on ancient yogi knowledge that provides a path for truth seekers. I feel that this book helped me understand more about my Self, and helped in my relationship with my daughter, my ex-partner, and my current partner. Like all the texts I have included in this book, *Inner Engineering* came to me spontaneously, during a conversation I was having with a friend. While I am a seeker of truth, I have never sought out any particular text, doctrine, or wisdom, rather I let them come to me. From this book, I gained an understanding of the flow of energy within us, and how it is aligned with the universe. The geometry of the human energy system is a journey from conclusion to confusion to consciousness. When conclusions are destroyed, there is confusion – but being joyfully confused about everything in the universe is a good state to be in!

I have never been keen on meditation, yoga and so-called spiritual exercises or retreats. So many of them seem to be set up as a quick fix for life's problems, and I wonder how many people who attend them actually go through the real path of seeking truth. If more of us really did seek the truth of life, we would live in a conscious world without bias, judgement, superiority, or arrogance. However, one weekend in 2019, I tried meditation for the first time. Thanks to the simple explanation in *Inner Engineering* I became aware of the movement of energy within me, simply through my own breathing – how it changed as it flowed from my chest to my abdomen – by facing palms up and down in sitting lotus posture. Without effort, I meditated for an hour and a half, took a brief break, and did so again. Altogether, over that weekend, I meditated for six hours. The experience surprised me and opened my eyes to the benefits of meditation, and it became a regular weekly and then daily practice. Throughout the coronavirus pandemic and lockdown, it has been something I did daily. I am so grateful for the experience, how it increases my awareness of the energies within my body and enables self-transformation.

'Inner Engineering' is the book that set me on that path. It has also helped me understand some of the buzzwords that we throw around in the corporate world, on social media, and even in our day-to-day lives without necessarily thinking about their true meaning. Awareness. Responsibility. Consciousness. Diversity. Inclusion. Purpose. Identity. Equality. Spirituality. Enlightenment. Awakening. Yoga. Meditation.

In learning the meaning of, and the distinction between, Identity, Intellect and Consciousness, I gained a better understanding of how thought and emotion create a conflict between our head and heart. Thought has a certain clarity, whereas with emotion that takes time. The distinction between 'me' and 'my mind' is the first step to freedom. Understanding how our mind functions (including our intellect, memory, awareness, and ego) enables us to better handle stress and anxiety, through an awareness of Self. Awareness is not something that we *do*, awareness is what we *are*. Once we are in touch with our awareness, we don't have to try to accomplish anything. The best possible thing that can happen to us, will happen.

The aim of every individual life is to touch the infinite – it is at the very core of our making. The science of yoga brings us into perfect alignment with all existence, through our physical body, intelligence, emotions, and energies. The universe is just a play of five elements (water, fire, earth, air, and ether) and we are nothing but energy. Understanding how the energies flow in our body through channels and chakras will give us an understanding of how to deal with physical, psychological, and emotional processes.

Guru literally means dispelled of darkness. The function of a guru is not to teach, indoctrinate or convert. The guru is here to throw light on dimensions beyond your sensory perceptions and your psychological drama, dimensions that you are currently unable to perceive. The guru is here fundamentally to throw light on the very nature of your existence. The solution for all the ills that plague humanity is self-transformation. Self-transformation is achieved not by morals or ethics or attitudinal or behavioural changes, but by experiencing the limitless nature of Who We Are. Self-transformation means nothing of the old remains. It is a dimensional shift in the way you perceive and experience life.

Wellbeing is a deep sense of pleasantness within. Body pleasantness is health; being very pleasant is a pleasure. Mind pleasantness is peace; being very pleasant is joy. Emotions pleasantness is love; being very pleasant is compassion. Life energies are bliss; being very pleasant is ecstasy. This is all you are seeking pleasantness within and without. When pleasantness is about within it is termed peace, joy, and happiness. When your surroundings become pleasant, it gets branded success. So essentially all human experience is only a question of pleasantness and unpleasantness in varying degrees.

Responsibility - It does not mean taking on burdens of the world, accepting blame for things you have done or not done, living in a state of guilt. Responsibility simply means your ability to respond. Deciding on I am responsible you have the ability to respond; I am not responsible you will not have the ability to respond. All it requires is for you to realise that you are responsible for all that you are and all that you are not, all that may happen to you and all that may not happen to you. Responsibility is about awareness, consciousness, and freedom; Reaction is about unawareness, unconsciousness, and enslavement. Your ability to respond is the way you are. Your ability to act relates to the outside world. Responsibility is not about action, but a way of being. Love is not something you do; it is just the way you are. My ability to respond is limitless, but my ability to act is limited. I am responsible for everything I am and everything I am not, for my capacities and my incapacities, for my joys and miseries. I am the one who determines the nature of my experience in this life and beyond. Conscious response brings you to a profound and enduring state of connectedness with life. Not as an idea or an emotion, but life as life is. Just willingness nothing else takes you to the very source of creation.

Yoga - The science of yoga is being in perfect alignment, in absolute harmony, in complete sync with existence. Yoga means Union. When in yoga your experiences, everything has become one. Yoga should bring you to an experience wherein if you sit here, there is no such thing as You and Me. It is all me or all you.

Karma Yoga or the yoga of action, you Molloy your physical body to reach ultimate union.

Gnana Yoga or the yoga of intelligence, you employ your intelligence to reach your ultimate nature.

Bhakti Yoga or the yoga of devotion, you employ your emotions to reach your ultimate nature.

Kriya Yoga or the yoga of transforming energies, you use your energies to reach the supreme experience.

All these aspects of action, intelligence, devotion and transformation must function in an integrated way if one wants to get anywhere. Focus is on Body, Mind, Emotion and Energy.

The system of yoga is a technology to create a distinction between you and your mind. There is a space between you and what you have gathered in terms of body and mind. Becoming conscious of this space is the first step to freedom. There are only two forms of suffering in this world: Physical and Mental. If you can be constantly conscious of the space between you and the body-mind, you have reached the end of suffering. You can BE and still choose to think or not think.

Stress - It is our compulsive reaction to the situations in which we are placed that causes stress. Stress is a certain level of internal friction. Stress is not because of work; no job is stressful, and many jobs could present challenging situations. Our inability to handle our own system that is stressing us.

Sexuality - It is psychological, if it is in your body, it is fine and beautiful. The moment it enters your mind it becomes an obsession and perversion. Of all the loving acts two human beings are capable of, the simple act of holding hands can often become the most intimate. The nature of the hands and feet is such that the energy system finds expression in these two parts of the body in a very singular way. The right represents Masculine - solar (Yin); Left represents Feminine - lunar (Yang).

Human Mind - it is manufacturing a million ways to suffer. Once you are no longer identified with your mind, you are free to be experience life beyond limitations. Being a Buddha means you have become a witness to your own intellect, who has transcended intellect, discriminatory and logical dimensions of life.

Intellect (Buddhi) - Gets identified with something, you function within the realm of this identity. Whatever you are identified with, all your thoughts and emotions spring from that identity. If you don't encumber your intellect with any identifications such as body, gender, family, qualifications, society, race, caste, creed, community, nation, even species then you travel naturally toward your ultimate nature.

Mind - To understand mind we need to investigate 16 dimensions of mind, which fall into four categories. Intellect is a discerning or discriminatory dimensions of the mind. Memory is the accumulative dimension of the mind, gathers information. Intelligence is the awareness which is beyond both intellect and memory. Ego is the aspect of mind from which you derive your senses of identity. Intellect is crucial for your survival. But intellect is becoming a barrier because you keep it constantly dipped in the accumulative part of the mind which is your memory. The accumulative part of the mind is merely a heap of impressions gathered from outside. Anybody, you encounter places something in your head and moves on; parents, teachers, friends, enemies, preachers, news, tv and so on. Information your mind receives enters you only through five sense organs. Sense organs always perceive everything only in comparison, there is always a duality. Human perception through the sense organs gives you an illusion of completeness but never comprehend the whole. If you soak your intellect in your awareness, the discerning dimension of your mind can turn into a tool of liberation, slice through what is true and untrue and deliver you to a different dimension of life altogether.

Awareness - It is not something that you do, Awareness is what you are. Awareness is aliveness and intelligence that is completely unsullied by memory. This is the deepest dimension of the mind and one that connects you with that which is the very basis of creation. Sleep, wakefulness, death are all just different levels of awareness. Awareness is a process of inclusiveness. A way of embracing this entire universe is by keeping your body, thoughts, emotion, and energies properly aligned, the awareness will blossom. When you are consciously in touch with your awareness, you gain access to the subtle dimension of physicality or akash (Ether). The universe is just a play of five elements water, fire, earth, air and ether. Once you are in touch with your awareness, you don't have to try to accomplish anything. The best possible thing that can happen to you will happen. Once you distance yourself from the compulsiveness of your own genetic and karmic information, life becomes unburdened, flexible, incredibly effortless. This is a dimension beyond intellect, beyond identification, memory, judgement, karma, beyond divisions of every kind. This is the intelligence of existence itself, in which life always happen exactly the way it should with ease. Knowledge is essentially accumulated information. All the information is related to the physical nature of existence; Knowing on other hand is a living intelligence with or with you, it still is. You are either in it or you are not, that is the only choice you have. The spiritual process is always a quest. Believing means you have assumed something that you do not know; Seeking means you have realised that you do not know.

A limited identity that we impose upon ourselves is what sets us up as Me versus the Others. It is in this space of division and separation that all the negativity is born. First, explore what it is that you really want. Once that is clear and you are committed to creating it, you generate a continuous process of thought in that direction. Mind as a thought process or intellect has many dimensions: One is the logical aspect another is the deeper emotional aspect. The deeper dimension of the mind is conventionally known as the Heart. The emotional mind is known as Manas. Manas is a complex amalgam of memory that moulds emotions. The way you feel and the way you think are both activities of the mind. The way you think is the way you feel but thought and feeling seem to be different in your experience.

Thoughts - Is just information that you have gathered and recycled. The most beautiful moments in your life, were the moments when you were not thinking about anything. You were just being. Thought has certain clarity, certain agility about it. Whereas Emotion is slower. Thought and emotion create conflict between head and heart. Emotion is just the juicier part of the thought. Largely the thought that leads to emotion. Thought and emotion are like sugar cane and its juice. Thought is not as intense as emotion in most people experience. People whose thought is very deep and don't have many emotions are very deep thinkers.

Devotion - This means dropping the dualities of like and dislike, attachment and aversion. It means everything is fine, God is everything or everything is God. By this, he or she arrives at a deep state of acceptance that is transformative and liberating. All-encompassing and all-inclusive; it doesn't discriminate. The path of knowing is harder, but it is an eyes-open path. Devotion is an eyes-closed path. For most people, emotion is more intense than thought. That is why devotion has been glorified above all other paths.

Love - Is a quality, not something to do with somebody else. Every action that we do is in some way to fulfil certain needs. People have physical, psychological, emotional, financial and social needs to fulfil. Don't fool yourself into believing that the relationships you have made for convenience, comfort and well-being are relationships of love. The moment there is a condition, it just amounts to a transaction. Maybe convenient transaction and arrangement. Love need not necessarily be convenient, most of the time it is not. It takes life, you must invest yourself. A love affair need not be with any person, you could be having a great love affair with life itself.

Energy - The sole aim of every individual life energy is to touch the infinite, the very core of our making. Life energies are always longing to break the boundaries set by your physical (body) and mental (mind) structures. The content of physical and mental bodies has been gathered from outside. They belong to you, but they are not you. Manage body and mind consciously, then your experience of life is hundred percent of your making.

All you need to do is create a distance between you and everything that you accumulated from outside. Pain is a natural phenomenon, but suffering is entirely self-created. Every human being has the choice, to suffer or not to suffer.

Karma - It means action. It could be in terms of the body, mind or energy. Transformation in life happens if you break the cyclical patterns of karma. The residue left by karma forms a pattern of its own gathering impressions and then into tendencies. These recurring memory patterns forms your life cycle which needs to be broken.

Kriya - It means internal action. Body is the accumulation of food; Mind is the accumulation of ideas. Even the imprints upon the energy body are an accumulation of the impressions of the five senses. Your ability to perform an action with the non-physical aspect of your energy is Kriya. Karma is your actions find outward expression involving body, mind and the physical dimensions of energy. If you turn inward and perform an action beyond all dimensions of physicality is Kriya. Karma is the process of binding you; Kriya is the process of liberating you. How do you access the non-physical aspect of your life energy - It is by aligning the physical, mental and energy body you find access to dimensions beyond the physical. If you want to hit the peak of your consciousness, discipline is essential. Discipline into all physical, psychological and emotional processes which is Kriya. You can't be partying till early morning and attempt to climb Mt Everest or finish a full marathon.

Human energy in our body - There are 72,000 channels (Nadis) where the energy moves in our system. The three basic channels are, Right is Pingala, Left is Ida and Central is Sushumna. Pingala symbolise masculine and Ida symbolise feminine, not from biological differences but by qualities. Pingala is very pronounced, outgoing, exploratory qualities represent the logical dimension (Sun). Ida is receptive and reflective qualities represent the intuitive dimension (Moon). Whether one is a man or woman has nothing to do with this. The human being is complete only when both masculine and feminine function at full force and are in proper balance. Central Nadi is independent of the 72,000 nadis. Once energies enter Sushumna your inner way of being becomes independent of the outside. Kundalini is energy and referred to as a coiled cobra because this energy exists within each human being, but until it moves you never realise it is there.

Chakras - Means wheel, and powerful centres in the physiology where the channels meet in a particular way to create an energy vortex. They meet in the form of a triangle. There are 114 chakras of which 112 are within the body and the other 2 outside. The major seven chakras with dominant life energies are; Muladhara located at perineum the space between anal outlet and genitals, represent food and sleep energies. Swadhishthana above the genital organs represents the pleasure energies. Manipuraka 3/4 of an inch below navel, represents as a doer. Anahata below where the ribcage meets diaphragm, represents a creative person. Vishuddhi at the pit of the throat, represents a powerful presence. Agna between eyebrows, is intellectually realised. Sahasrara is on top of the head, is reaching a higher state.

Mula, Swadhi, Mani are concerned with keeping the body stable and rooted. Earthly qualities with the grip of nature. Upper chakras Vishu, Agna, Sahas are centres that draw you away from the pull of the earth. Longing for infinite. Anahata is the balance between survival instincts and the instinct toward liberation. Reaching Sahasrara your experience is no longer intellectual, it is experiential. Samadhi is a certain stage of equanimity in which the intellect goes beyond its normal function of discrimination.

Tantra Means technology. It is a certain capability; if you have no tantra in you, you have no technology to transform people, all you have are words. Words can be inspirational and directional but not transformative.

Human consciousness is missing in our world. Everything else is in place but the human being is not in place. Your joy, misery, love, agony, bliss lie in your hands. There is a way out, and the way out is in.

Inner Engineering Modules - Summary of what I learnt - Perceive you know; rest is imagination. Expand your imagination. Desire is a source of misery in life, fulfilled and unfulfilled desire. The body never lies as Mind does. Desire is life and fear of suffering. Desire can be in a conscious state (straight) and or compulsive state (circles). Understand desire; choose well. Desire not for more, but all. Distinguish between what is You and your Ego, what are you and your shadow? Who am I and what is the nature of my existence. Responsibility is our choice and willingness. Karma is action, being responsible is the nature of life. Right now (moment) is inevitable. Moment to moment of self-awareness, Happiness pleasantness is acceptance (full) of the moment (what is there). Stupid mind is not in the moment, always in past and future leads to hallucinating, pain and suffering. The cause and effect; likes and dislikes. A drop in the ocean has the ocean in it like drop in the ocean. Existence is in you as you are part of existence. Eat by choice and not by compulsion, understand the needs of your body. Understand three types of food-related to positive, negative energies and balanced. The basic sound of creation and root of physical existence is AUM. Truth can only be perceived or experienced. Silence is the basis of all sound. Create what you want. Nothing repeats in existence, only mind and memory repeats. Time is a relative experience and love is who you are.

My responsibility is limitless. This moment is Inevitable. This mind and body are gathering and not me.

One day, a monk was sitting down under a tree. After a long day walking, a tree was a pleasant place to sit under rather than sitting in harsh sun. An astrologer of great proficiency in his trade came for a bath in the river and saw a footprint on the riverbank. There are observations through which by looking at the way one's feet are, someone can predict exactly what he will do. He saw that this is the footprint of an emperor, someone who should rule the world. Then he wondered, why would such a person be in this remote place? And he followed the footprint, thinking he will meet an emperor. Then he saw this monk, sitting under a tree. He looked at this and thought, "Either my astrology has gone all wrong, or I am being fooled, or I am in some kind of hallucination. What's happening here?" He went to Monk and asked, "Who are you?" Monk said, "I am nobody, I am just a nobody." "But you have the feet of an emperor, you should conquer the world!" Monk said, "That I will, but not by conquest."

There are two ways you can have the world – either by conquest or by inclusion. Both ways something or someone becomes yours. But if you go by conquest, it will always be a painful and loss. If you choose by inclusion, this will become a great enhancement of life. He said, "I am the emperor of the world." The astrologer said, "You are a monk, you own nothing." "I own nothing, and I am a nobody. That is why everything is mine."

Becoming a nothing does not mean that you are no use, when you are a no-thing, it means that you have become all inclusive. If you are something, it means that you can only be that. If you are a no-thing, you can be any way you want. This astrologer sat down and said, "You are a monk, you have nothing, on top of it you say, 'I am a nobody and everything is mine.' What is this?" Monk said, "You are busy making predictions of life, instead of having a plan." You make predictions of life because you are incapable of planning. That is why you fall back on predictions. If you are capable of making a plan and executing it, you would not fall back on predictions.

CHAPTER FOUR

Acceptance, Silence and Inner Peace

A deep dive into understanding the True Self

I had a serious health problem in late 2018 and it took me six months to recover. Up until September of that year, I was fine – in fact, in the twelve months prior I'd completed six half-marathons (21.1 km) and was preparing to attempt my first full marathon (42.2 km). My illness started with symptoms that felt like a cold or flu, so I just took paracetamol and carried on. After a while, other symptoms began to appear – fever, swollen lymph nodes and general fatigue. Finally, I listened to my body and saw a doctor. From there, I was sent for blood tests, ultrasounds, CT scans, urine tests, and chest x-rays. The tests showed that there was an infection in my abdomen but gave no indication of what caused it. The doctors ruled out tuberculosis, cancer, a bacterial infection, or anything neurological... even though by now I was having problems with my vision as well. Even after treatment for my vision and biopsies on my lymph nodes, I still didn't have any answers as to the cause of my ill health.

While going through all these tests and appointments, I was still running. I had signed up for a half marathon well in advance, and with permission from my doctors decided I still needed to run it. Initially, I just wanted to finish, but by listening to my body and challenging my mind, I completed the course in a reasonable two and a half hours. Following the run, I was recommended to another specialist for yet more, high-level blood tests. I was experiencing regular nightly fevers and loss of appetite. I actually started to believe that maybe now was the time to leave my body in peace.

From these new, intensive tests, the specialist was finally able to identify a serious viral infection. I was immediately admitted to the hospital, where I was hooked up to a PICC line. A very thin tube was inserted into the vein in my right arm and all the way to the larger veins close to my heart. Thanks to the PICC line, the necessary medication could be fed directly to my heart, where it could repair my blood. This procedure was done under a local anaesthetic, and I can vividly recall talking to the nurse about the beauty of life while the line was being inserted from my arm to my heart. It was honestly a moment of true peace.

To continue my treatment and recovery, I had a permanent intravenous drip attached to deliver antibiotics into my system. I got approval from the doctors to continue going to work, as my condition was not contagious to others, and would wear the antibiotic drip hidden beneath my business suit. Through this time, I could only sleep in one position and depended on help from my partner to get dressed. Daily treatment continued until January 2019, my check-ups until May, and I closed this journey with one last surgery in that month. Meanwhile, I continued my running, and finally completed my first full marathon in October 2019.

After getting the all-clear, I visited India in July. There, I returned to Varanasi for the third time. My first trip, in 1999, was to help me recover after I took sleeping pills, got on a train and tried to disappear. While I don't remember anything from that time, apart from taking a dip in the Ganges, I know that I was a lost soul. My second trip, in 2015, was in response to a calling. All the events in my life to this point – the loss of my mother to cancer, the process of IVF, the breakup of my relationship with my ex-partner and separation from my daughter, being scammed by business partners into near-bankruptcy – ignited a longing within me to return. But more than that, I felt called to Varanasi, and the truth as well. The trip itself was effortless, with none of the difficulties that usually arise when travelling from South India to North India at the peak of winter. My third trip, in 2019, exactly twenty years from my first visit, felt like a witnessing. Every aspect of that journey I witnessed in peace, because I had reached the Source. The Source is understanding my True Self. It is consciousness and a constant state of pleasantness. The Source is within one's own Self – the rest is seeking. The Source is in our heart, where we all meet as one and don't judge.

I know this recent trip to Varanasi will not be my last. I still see it every day, images and memories rising to the quiet surface of my mind. Within me, there is a deep call to return. I look forward to what that next trip will bring.

A story about death I relate with, a mother of three young boys lost her husband and was grief-stricken. Naturally, after this she clung on to the three children as her life. But the eldest boy also died after a year, and soon after, the second one also passed away. Now she clung on to her only child for dear life, but this boy also died soon after. Unable to bear this, she took the little boy's body and went to the Buddha. She said, "You and all your spirituality. Whatever you are talking does not mean anything unless you bring this boy to life. My husband died, and I somehow bore that. My first boy died and then the second one, too; I still held on. Now the last one is also gone. If you are real, prove it now by bringing this boy to life."

Buddha looked at the woman and knew that in this state of inflamed emotion, whatever he could say or do would not get across. So, he said, "I will bring your boy back to life. Go and get me a few sesame seeds from a house that has never known death." Carrying the boy's body, the woman went from house to house, looking for one that had never known death. After going through the entire town, she realized there wasn't a single home like this.

Then she stopped, did what she had to do with the body, came back and sat in front of Buddha. She remained with him right through her life and followed the path of spiritual enlightenment.

During my health scare, while I endured a lot of pain, I didn't suffer. I read and reflected on the teachings of Ramana Maharshi. In *Who Am I?* he explores the nature of self-enquiry through a set of questions and answers, and in *Be As You Are*, he recounts conversations he's had with the many seekers of truth who visit his ashram for guidance. Those six months could have had a serious impact on my mental health, relationships, work and overall life, but at the time my mind was calm. I was somehow aware there was no point in fighting the situation. I accepted my life for what it was, with all the uncertainty it might bring, and that gave me interior peace.

Ramana Maharshi explains the nature of our mind and the difference between True Self and Ego. For him, our minds *are* our thoughts, and it is these thoughts that create our world. Nothing else exists. When we sleep without dreams, our so-called world doesn't exist. Nothing we have identified with exists: loved ones, work, family, friends, money, favourites, likes and dislikes, everything disappears...until we wake up and open our eyes. This is what our mind does, it creates our own unique projection of the world. But what if our thoughts are governed by Ego rather than our True Self? What impact does that have on our view of the world?

Of course, we need the mind to survive, just like any other animal on the planet. But humans who have their basic needs met should be able to access the consciousness within us – our True Self. All of us are searching, driven by a deep thirst, but so often the water we think we've found turns out to be a mirage. One after the other, we chase mirages, unable to quench our thirst. But what we are looking for is already within us. We are the ocean, and our mind and body are merely a drop of water within it. Just like this, we are at once a part of the universe, in the universe, and the universe is in us too. The teachings of Ramana Maharshi can be very deep for beginners, but once we place our Ego aside and read with absolute openness, we will start to see the meaning of life and the True Self.

Even though I endured so much physical pain, whether, through my long-distance running or my health issues, I could handle it with awareness, through a separation of myself from my mind. I learned that we have this awareness within us, this ability to view the world as though sleeping, without any duality, bias, judgement, or boundaries. I refused to allow my mind to engage in an emotional reaction, creating drama as our minds so often try to do, instead I realised that this was just another moment in life. I would pass through it, like a cloud.

A story about, how should I deal with the pain and suffering in life. There was a student who sought the wisdom of a great sage, hoping to find a way to escape his pain & suffering. The sage looked at the man and said, 'I will help you, but first, you must do something for me. Take this spoon, fill it with oil, and walk through the town without spilling a drop.' The man thought this task was simple enough and agreed. He took the spoon, filled it with oil, and began to walk through the town. As he carefully balanced the spoon, he couldn't help but focus all his attention on not spilling any oil.

When he returned to the sage, the sage asked, 'Did you see the beautiful flowers in the town square? Did you notice the children playing and the laughter of families?'

The man realized he had been so fixated on the spoon that he hadn't noticed anything else. The sage then said, this is the key to dealing with pain. Just as you were so focused on the spoon that you missed the beauty around you, when you are consumed by your suffering, you miss the beauty of life.

Pain is like the spoon, and life is like the town. Don't let the pain consume your entire focus. Remember to look around and appreciate the beauty that still exists. The student understood the sage's message: while pain and suffering are part of life, it's essential not to let them overshadow the beauty and joy that can be found in every moment. This story serves as a reminder that even in the face of pain, there is an opportunity to find meaning and beauty in life.

In this digital age of constant connection, silence has become a precious commodity. Silence allows us to focus on inner calm and helps us connect with our True Self. According to Ramana Maharshi, silence is the best and the most potent initiation. Silence is ever speaking, silence is never-ending speech, silence is the true teaching, suited only for the most advanced seeker. The state which transcends speech and thought is silence. In silence, we find truth and become connected with our True Self.

Before my incident with the pills and the train (which I shared in Chapter One) I sought to self-harm, to distract myself from the pain I was feeling in my heart. I walked to the outskirts of the town where I was living, found a statue of Hanuman (the Hindu monkey god) and sat beneath its shadow. There, I lit a candle. I felt that the chaos within me, and my disconnect from my family and society, were more painful than any flame – so I began to burn my left hand. In silence, I simply weighed the pain of the flesh against the pain of the heart. Every week for three months, I continued to harm myself this way. And now, the scar that remains on my left hand silently reminds me that I have been searching and seeking peace all along. Now, I know the pain I felt back then was not in my heart, but from my mind.

When he was young, Ramana Maharshi journeyed into such a deep meditative state (leaving his body and mind) that he did not feel it when rats started eating the flesh on his legs. He wasn't aware until a passer-by noticed and took him for medical treatment. I am not a sage-like him. What I knew back then was a drop in the ocean, what I know now is still a drop in the ocean. But now, at least, I know what I don't know – and that's progress.

I have handled the events of my life in my own silence. I was my own friend, my own enemy, my own god, and my own devil. Silence speaks to my True Self and nature, to the thief in me and the Buddha in me. Silence has taken me on this journey of self-enquiry, and it is a part of my path towards truth – all things lead to my understanding of the difference between my True Self and my mind and body.

My human design is made up of two distinct energies, a Martyr, who learns through trial and error, and a heretic with opinions and beliefs opposite to the majority. The martyr energy leads to life full of experiences and experiments. Meaning to face challenges in life that gain wisdom and insight. My life may seem chaotic, but it is crucial for the wisdom I gained and able to share with others. The journey towards self-understanding is crucial for me and is rich with full of learning and growth. My journey to learn the secret of happiness, like the story from the book The Alchemist.

A merchant sent his son to learn the Secret of Happiness from the wisest of men. The young man wandered through the desert for forty days until he reached a beautiful castle at the top of a mountain. There lived the sage that the young man was looking for. However, instead of finding a holy man, our hero entered a room and saw a great deal of activity; merchants coming and going, people chatting in the corners, a small orchestra playing sweet melodies, and there was a table laden with the most delectable dishes of that part of the world. The wise man talked to everybody, and the young man had to wait for two hours until it was time for his audience.

The Sage listened attentively to the reason for the boy's visit but told him that at that moment he did not have the time to explain to him the Secret of Happiness. He suggested that the young man take a stroll around his palace and come back in two hours' time. "However, I want to ask you a favour," he added, handling the boy a teaspoon, in which he poured two drops of oil. "While you walk, carry this spoon and don't let the oil spill." The young man began to climb up and down the palace staircases, always keeping his eyes fixed on the spoon. At the end of two hours, he returned to the presence of the wise man.

"So," asked the sage, "did you see the Persian tapestries hanging in my dining room? Did you see the garden that the Master of Gardeners took ten years to create? Did you notice the beautiful parchments in my library?"

Embarrassed, the young man confessed that he had seen nothing. His only concern was not to spill the drops of oil that the wise man had entrusted to him.

"So, go back and see the wonders of my world," said the wise man. "You can't trust a man if you don't know his house." Now more at ease, the young man took the spoon and strolled again through the palace, this time paying attention to all the works of art that hung from the ceiling and walls. He saw the gardens, the mountains all around the palace, the delicacy of the flowers, the taste with which each work of art was placed in its niche. Returning to the sage, he reported in detail all that he had seen. "But where are the two drops of oil that I entrusted to you?" asked the sage. Looking down at the spoon, the young man realized that he had spilled the oil.

"Well, that is the only advice I have to give you," said the sage of sages. "The Secret of Happiness lies in looking at all the wonders of the world and never forgetting the two drops of oil in the spoon."

Ramana Maharshi considered the Self to be permanent and enduring, surviving physical death. When we persistently enquire into the nature of the mind, the mind will end, leaving the Self as the residue – our real nature is liberation. The habits of the mind are obstacles which hinder the realisation of the Self. We play roles on the stage of life, but we must not identify ourselves with those parts. Ego is the thought 'I', but the true 'I' is the Self. Through self-inquiry, we must distinguish between the pure 'I', and the 'I' thought. Day-to-day activities don't stand in the way of inaction and peace of mind, we can remain as a silent witness to all the activities taking place. Time exists only in our mind, it is an idea that appears after the Ego arises, but the True Self is beyond time and space.

When he answers the question, 'Who Am I?' Ramana Maharshi says the gross body is composed of seven fundamental functions. However: I am not the five senses of hearing, touch, sight, taste, smell. I am not their respective objects of sound, touch, colour, taste and odour. I am not the five cognitive senses of speech, locomotion, grasping, excretion and procreation. Or their respective functions of speaking, moving, grasping, excreting and enjoying. I am not the five functions of breathing or vital air (Vayu). The Sanskrit word 'Vayu' means wind and the root 'Va' translates to That which flows. Thus, Vayu is an energetic force that moves in a specific direction to control bodily functions and activities. The primary currents of the vital force of air, or the five life forces relates to five elements,

Forward moving air, situated in the heart and chest, moves all around; action is crystallization; element is air. The air that moves away, situated in the pelvic floor moves downward; action is elimination; element is earth. The balancing air, situated in the abdomen with its energy centred in the navel moves inward; action is assimilation; element is fire. That which carries upward. Situated in the throat, it has a circular flow around the neck and head moves upward; action is metabolizing; element is ether. Outward moving air, situated in the heart and lungs moves outward; action is circulation; element is water.

I am not even the mind which thinks. I am not the nescience (residual knowledge or lack of knowledge). Our body and mind can carry residual knowledge from the activities mentioned above, which is endowed only with the residual impression of objects. I am not where there are no objects or nothing functioning.

If I am none of these, then who am I? After removing everything 'I am not', awareness alone remains. That *I Am*. In other words, by ruling out the things that we strongly identify ourselves with, like our name, title, position, power, money, brother, sister, mother, father, children, religion, caste, creed, race, ideology, place, city, country, sports team and so on, we will get closer to our True Self.

When you ask another human being, 'who are you?' the answer is usually something they have identified with, a name, title, ethnicity, country, etc. Not many would know the true answer. We live in a society and a world where most of us aren't guided to a deeper understanding of 'who I am'. Our strong attachment to worldly things, the way we use them to create our identity, can make it difficult to reach an understanding of the True Self. But if we are loyal to ourselves, we will take the time to know our Self. This is the key we need to open inwardness so that the chaos within us will disappear. Nothing in this world is more personal than the True Self, nothing more pleasant than the True Self, nothing more blissful than the True Self.

I would like to remind you that Ramana Maharshi's teachings can be very deep. The best way to read this final chapter is as a child with no knowledge, learning for the first time about life and Self. As an adult, with our accumulation of knowledge, experiences and judgements, it can be challenging to understand this chapter. If we are truly seeking to understand our own Self, then *Be As You Are* is the answer I have found. It has certainly given me more clarity about my Self and helped in my understanding of the world.

Life takes care of life itself. The inequality I saw as a child, the disconnect and chaos I endured as a young man, the relationship loss, and the health concerns I faced as an adult, all led to a reckoning for me, to seek for truth. The boy in me now is saying: the world is the way it is. The young version of me is now saying: I am the universe, and everything is connected. The adult me is saying: death is just your True Self leaving the mind and body. There is no death for your True Self.

This moment tells me: I am the river. I travel through peaks, mountains, forests, villages, and cities before I reach the ocean. And then, I become the ocean. This moment is saying to all of us: let life take care of you, all you need to do is live consciously. The thought of changing our habits, both personal and in business, can appear daunting. But taking a moment to improve the way we do things can reap great rewards. The bliss of knowing the Self is always in you. You will find it for yourself if you seek it earnestly. It is all about our perception versus perspective, just like the story of the elephant and blind men.

There lived a group of blind men who had always wondered about a creature called an elephant. These blind men had heard many stories about elephants, but since they couldn't see, they didn't really know what an elephant was like. One day, the blind men heard that a mighty elephant was passing by their village. Excited and curious, they decided to go and find it. Imagine their surprise when they finally did! Standing right there in front of them was this enormous, strange creature. "This must be the elephant!" they exclaimed.

The blind men reached out with their hands to explore this magnificent animal. The first blind man touched the side of the elephant. "Aha!" he cried. "An elephant is solid and sturdy, like a great wall!"

The second blind man felt the elephant's tusk. "Hmm," he said, "this feels sharp and smooth, very much like a powerful spear!"

The third blind man reached for the elephant's trunk. "Aha!" he exclaimed. "It's clear to me now. An elephant is long and wiggly like a giant snake!"

The rest of the blind men eagerly explored the elephant, each one touching a different part. One thought the elephant's leg was like a sturdy tree trunk. Another felt the ear and declared that an elephant was broad and floppy, like a big fan. Even the elephant's tail was described as a long, thin rope!

After touching different parts, the blind men started to talk about what they had found. "This elephant is mighty like a wall," said the first blind man.

"No, no!" insisted the second," it's more like a spear!"

"You must be mistaken," said the third man. "Surely, an elephant is like a giant snake."

The blind men continued arguing over each other. Each one was so sure that their own experience was the only right one! They argued and argued, their voices growing louder. It seemed like they would never come to an understanding.

A wise old man passing by who had been watching the argument felt it was time to step in. He smiled gently at the blind men. "Friends," he said, "why are you arguing?"

"We all can't be right about how an elephant is like," grumbled one of the blind men.

The wise old man nodded. "You each touched a different part of the elephant, so it's no wonder your ideas are different. But you are each partially correct, too."

The old man continued, "An elephant is indeed like a wall, a spear, a snake, a tree, a fan, and even a rope. This amazing creature has all those features and more!"

The blind men listened carefully and began to understand. Each one had experienced only a part of the magnificent elephant. It dawned on them that to truly understand something, sometimes you need to take a step back and consider the whole picture. This is about understanding the bigger picture. The world is a big and complex place. Often, we only see a piece of a larger puzzle, just like the blind men and the elephant. It's important to listen to the ideas of others and try to see the world from different perspectives. That's how we grow wiser and discover the truth! This story tells us about the reality of life and about a basic problem that we all have. It tells us that individual truth may be partially true, but it is not the ultimate truth. The moral of the story is that there might be some fact to what somebody says. We might not agree with it at first because we have our own reasons. But what we think might not be the absolute truth.

The following quotes from different passages of the book *Be As You Are* - The teachings of Ramana Maharshi by David Godman.

The Self - The real self or real 'I' is contrary to perceptible experience, not an experience of individuality but a non-personal, all-inclusive awareness. It is not to be confused with the individual self, which was essentially non-existent, being a fabrication of the mind, which obscures the true experience of the Real Self. The real self is always present and always experienced, only consciously aware of it as it really is when the self-limiting tendencies of the mind have created. Permanent and continuous self-awareness is known as self-realisation. The self is a pure being, subjective awareness of 'I Am' which is completely devoid of the feeling 'I Am This' or 'I Am That' there are no objects or subjects in the self, there is only an awareness of being. This awareness is consciousness, a state of unbroken happiness.

Reality - Reality must be always real. It is not with forms and names. It is not bound; it is beyond the expressions. The radiance of consciousness, in the form of awareness within and without, is the primal reality. Its form is silence.

Awareness - You are awareness, awareness is another name for you. There is no need to attain or cultivate it. All you have to do is to give up being aware of other things, that is of the non-self. If one gives up being aware of them then pure awareness alone remains and that is the self.

Silence - The state which transcends speech and thought is silence. The state in which the thought 'I' (The Ego) doesn't rise even in the least, alone is self which is silence.

Body - The world doesn't exist without the body, the body never exists without the mind, the mind never exists without consciousness and consciousness never exists without reality. Dig a hole and create a huge pit, the space in the pit or hole hasn't been created by us. We have just removed the earth which was filling the space there. Space was there then and is also there now.

Liberation - It is our very nature. The very fact that we wish for liberation shows that freedom from all bondage is our real nature.

The three states are wakefulness, dream, and deep sleep. If you remain as you are now, you are in the wakeful state, this becomes hidden in the dream state and the dream state disappears when you are in deep sleep. The three states come and go, but you are always there. It is like a cinema. The screen is always there but several types of pictures appear on the screen and then disappear. Ocean on the screen doesn't wet the screen, fire on screen doesn't burn the screen. All three states come and go, the self is not bothered, it has only one state like screen. Self alone exists as the screen, if you hold on to the self, you will not be deceived by the appearance of the pictures appear and disappear.

The Mind turned inwards is the self, turned outwards it becomes the ego and all the world. The self exists without the mind, never the mind without the self. The heart is the core of one's being, the centre without which there is nothing whatever. The heart is from which thoughts arise, on which they subsist and where they are resolved. The thoughts are the content of the mind, and they shape the universe. The heart is the centre of all. The consciousness which is the real existence, and which doesn't go out to know things which are other than self alone is the heart. Because you identify with the body, you see the world around you and say that the waking state is filled with interesting things. The sleep state appears dull because you were not there as an individual and therefore these things were not. There is the continuity of being in all three states, but no continuity of the individual and the objects. Therefore, the state of being is permanent and the body and the world are not.

The Ego self appears and disappears and is transitory, whereas the real self is permanent. Though you are the true self, you wrongly identify the real self with the ego-self. Take care of yourself, let the world take care of itself. See yourself. If you know the self there will be no darkness, no ignorance, and no misery. Knowing the self is being the self, being means existence, one's own existence. Our real nature is liberation. But we are imagining we are bound and are making various, strenuous attempts to become free, while we are all the while free.

The habits of mind are the obstacles which hinder the realisation of the self. Ego is the thought 'I' the true 'I' is the self. The state free from thoughts is the only real state. The idea of time is only in your mind, there is no time for the self. Time arises as an idea after the ego arises, but you are the self beyond time and space. You exist even in the absence of time and space. The bound man versus liberated one can be distinguished as the ordinary person who lives in the brain unaware of the self in the heart. He/she sees things outside him/herself, separate from the world. The person who was realised is aware of their own existence as one, as the real, the self in selves, in all things, eternal and immutable, in all that is is permanent and mutable. Pure consciousness of being is the heart. From heart arises 'I Am' ness as the primary point of one's experience.

The self alone is and nothing else. Differentiation is threefold owing to ignorance of the same kind, of a different kind and as parts in itself. The world is not another self-similar to the self. It is not different from the self, nor is it part of the self. Three states (waking, dream and sleep) are detachedly witnessed as Pictures superimposed, for the liberated person who is in the fourth state (wakeful sleep) which is beyond those 3 states. For the conscious all the three states are equally unreal, but for the ordinary unable to comprehend this, because for the ordinary the standard of reality is the waking state, whereas for the pure conscious the standard of reality is reality itself. This reality of pure consciousness is eternal by its nature and therefore subsists equally during waking, dreaming and sleep.

How the conscious person can live and act without the mind, although living and acting require the use of the mind. Just like the pottery wheel goes on turning round even after the potter has ceased to turn it because the pot is finished. And the electric fan goes on revolving for some time after we switch off the current. The predestined Karma which created the body will make it go through whatever activities it was meant for. A conscious person performs actions in some such a way as a child that is roused from sleep to eat, eats but doesn't remember the next morning what he/she ate. A child and a conscious person are similar in a way. Incidents interest a child only so long as they last. A child ceases to think of them after they have passed away. So, it is with conscious liberated one.

Nature of mind is nothing other than the 'I' thought. The mind and the ego are one and the same. Mind (Manas), Intellect (Buddhi), The storehouse of mental tendencies (chittam) and Ego (Ahamkara) all are only one mind itself. The 'I' thought is the all-important thought personality idea or thought is also the root or the stem of all other thoughts since each idea or thought arises only as someone's thought and is not known to exist independently of the Ego. The ego, therefore, exhibits thought activity. The second and third persons (he, she, you, that etc) don't appear except to the first person (I). Therefore, they arise only after the first person appears, so all the three persons seem to rise and sink together. Trace the ultimate cause of 'I' or personality. This is the pursuit of wisdom.

When the mind unceasingly investigates its own nature, it transpires that there is no such thing as mind. The mind is merely thoughts. Of all the thoughts the thought 'I' is the root. Therefore, the mind is only the thought 'I'. The ego functions as the knot between the self which is pure consciousness and the physical body which is inert and insentient (unable to understand). Self-enquiry must distinguish between the 'I' pure in itself and the 'I' thought. The latter being merely a thought sees subject, object, sleeps, wakes up, eats, thinks and dies and is reborn. But the pure 'I' is the pure being, eternal existence free from ignorance and thought illusion. In a cinema show, you can see pictures only in very dim light or in darkness. But when all the lights are switched on, the pictures disappear. If you stay as the 'I', your being alone, without thought, the 'I' thought will disappear and the delusion will vanish forever, just like the pictures and objects disappear at the cinema.

Self is beyond mind - when the room is dark a lamp is necessary to illuminate and eyes to cognise objects. But when the sun has risen there is no need for a lamp to see objects. To see the sun no lamp is necessary, it is enough that you turn your eyes towards the self-luminous sun. Similarly, with the mind, to see objects the reflected light of the mind is necessary. To see the heart, it is enough that the mind is turned towards it. Then the mind loses itself and the heart shines forth. The essence of the mind is only awareness or consciousness. When the ego, however, dominates it, it functions as the reasoning, thinking or sensing faculty. When the mind perishes in the supreme consciousness of one's own self, know that all the various powers beginning with the power of liking including the power of doing and knowing will entirely disappear, being found to be an unreal imagination appearing in one's own form of consciousness. The real 'I' in which the activity of thinking and forgetting has perished, alone is the pure liberation.

Self-enquiry and realisation - Both are the same if we are looking to define. Meditation requires an object to meditate upon, whereas there is only a subject without the object in self-enquiry. Mediation or concentration on an object fulfils the purpose of keeping away diverse thoughts and fixing the mind on a single thought, which must also disappear before realisation. The realisation is nothing new to be acquired. It is already there but obstructed by a screen of thoughts. All our attempts are directed to lifting this screen and then realisation is revealed.

The objective world is in the subjective consciousness. The mind turned outwards results in thoughts and objects, turned inwards it becomes itself the self. The degree of the absence of thoughts is the measure of your progress towards self-realisation. But self-realisation itself doesn't admit progress, it is ever the same. The self remains always in realisation. The obstacles are thoughts, progress is measured by the degree of removal of the obstacles to understanding that the self is always realised. The ego says many things and not you. Once born you reach something, if you reach it, you return also. Be as you are, see who you are and remains as the self, free from birth, going, coming and returning. You are aware of the self even though the self is not objectified. The wrong identity has forged the difficulty of not knowing the obvious self because it cannot be objectified.

Being - Your duty is to be and not to be this or that. 'I Am that I Am' sums up the whole truth. The truth of oneself alone is worthy to be scrutinised and known. This knowledge of oneself will be revealed only to the consciousness, which is silent, clear and free from the activity of the agitated suffering mind. Know that the consciousness which always shines in the heart as the formless self, 'I' and which is known by one's being still without thinking about anything as existent or non-existent, alone is a perfect reality.

Centre of the heart - when you realise you automatically feel that the centre is there. You can't know it with your mind. It is located on the right side of the chest and called the seat of consciousness. The self is the heart itself than to say that it is in the heart.

Pure consciousness is indivisible, it is without parts. It has no form and shape, no within and without. There is no right or left for it. The heart includes all and nothing is outside or apart from it. The body is itself a mere projection of the mind, and the mind is but a poor reflection of the radiant heart. Meditation is by you, of you and in you. It must go on where you are. It cannot be outside you. So, you are the centre of meditation and that is the heart. What remains all through deep sleep and waking is the same. But in waking there is unhappiness and the effort to remove it. Ask who wakes up from sleep you say 'I'. Heart the source, is the beginning the middle and the end of all. Heart the supreme space is never a form, it is the light of truth.

Surrender - It is enough that one surrenders oneself. Surrender is to give oneself up to the original cause of one's being. Don't delude yourself by imagining such a source to be some god outside you. Your source is within yourself. That means that you should seek the source and merge it.

Love - Love means one has love towards one's own self. Only if one knows the truth of love, which is the real nature of self, will the strong entangled know of life be united. Only if one attains the height of love will liberation be attained. The experience of self is only love, which is seeing only love, hearing only love, feeling only love, tasting only love and smelling only love which is bliss.

Worshipping the formless reality by unthought Thought is the best kind of worship. Formless worship is possible only for people who are devoid of the ego form. A true guru is someone who has realised the self and who is able to use his power to assist others towards the goal of self-realisation, guru means guri which is concentration. The self doesn't move, the world moves in it. You are only what you are, there is no change in you. The fact is that you are not the body. What looks like a departure from here and there and everywhere, these scenes shift. Be the self and the desires and doubts will disappear. Doubts arise because of the wrong outlook and consequent expectation of things external to oneself. Nothing is external to the self.

Silence - How does speech arise. First, there is abstract knowledge. Out of this arises the ego, which in turn gives rise to Thought and thought to the spoken word. So the word is the great-grandson or daughter of the original source. If the word can produce an effect, judge for yourself, how much more powerful must be through silence. Silence is the best and the most potent initiation, initiation by touch, look, teach etc are all a lower order. Language is only a medium for communicating one's thoughts to another. It is called in only after thoughts arise. 'I' thought is the root of all conversation. Silence is ever speaking, silence is never-ending speech, silence is the true teaching, suited only for the most advanced seeker. Others require words to explain the truth, but the truth is beyond words. It doesn't admit of explanation.

Pain or pleasure are aspects of the mind only. Essential nature is happiness. But we have forgotten the self and imagine that the body or the mind is the self. It is that wrong identity that gives rise to misery. The mental tendency is very ancient and has continued for innumerable past births, hence it has grown strong. Mediation is to focus on one thought. If a single thought prevails, all other thoughts are put off and finally eradicated. When the object of love prevails only good thoughts hold the field. No learning or knowledge of scriptures is necessary to know the self, as no person requires a mirror to see self.

The body itself is a projection of the mind. It is the mind which creates the body, the brain in it, and also ascertains that the brain is its seat.

Food - According to mental state food can be distinguished as, Sattvic means purity or harmony which includes dairy products, fruit, vegetables and cereals maintaining a still quiet mind. Rajas means activity which include meat, fish, hot spicy foods as chillies, onion, garlic result in an overactive mind. Tamas means sluggishness which include decayed state or product of fermentation lead to hampering clear decisive thinking.

Follow moderation in food, moderation in sleep and moderation in speech.

Awareness in worldly work the feeling 'I Work' is the hindrance, ask yourself 'Who Works' remember Who you are then your work will not bind you, it will go on automatically. Make no effort either to work or to renounce, it is your effort which is the bondage. What is destined to happen will happen. If you are destined not to work, work cannot be had even if you hunt for it. If you are destined to work, you will not be able to avoid it and you will be forced to engage yourself in it. So, leave it to the higher power (The Self), you cannot renounce or retain as you choose. Attending to the self means attending to the work. When you walk from one place to another you don't attend to the steps you take and yet you find yourself after a time at your goal. With all kinds of work that goes on without your attending to it like walking. Don't imagine it is you who are doing the work. Think that it is the underlying current hitch is doing it. Identify yourself with the current, if you work unhurriedly, with recollection then your work or service will not be a hindrance.

Solitude for self-enquiry, there is solitude everywhere. The individual is solitary always. His business is to find it out within, not to seek it outside the self. Solitude is in the mind of a human; one might be in the thick of the world and maintain the serenity of mind. Such a one is in solitude. Another may stay in the forest, but still unable to control his/her mind, solitude is a function of the mind. In silence and solitude either you can attain peace and connect with yourself or be restless and complain about the world.

A story of complaining, A monastery strict rule is a vow of silence, no one was allowed to speak at all. But there was one exception to this rule. Once every year, the monks were permitted to speak just two words.

After spending his first year at the monastery, one monk went to the master. "It has been one year, congratulations," said the master. "What are the two words you would like to say?"

"Bed Hard," said the monk. "I see," replied the master and gave some soft blankets to all monks.

Another year passed; the monk returned to the master. "It has been one more year," said the master. "What are the two words you would like to say?"

"Food Stinks," said the monk. "I see," replied the master and improved the quality of the food.

Yet another year passed, and the monk once again met with the master who asked, "What are your two words now, after these three years?"

"I Quit," said the monk. "I can see why; all you ever do is complain." replied the master.

A complaining mind is never peaceful.

Day to Day Activities - The activities of the wise exist only in the eyes of others and not in his/her own, although they may be accomplishing immense tasks, he/she really does nothing. Therefore, activities don't stand in the way of inaction and peace of mind. You remain a silent witness of all the activities taking place. Does a man who is acting on the stage in a female part forget that he is the man. Similarly, we too must play our parts on the stage of life, but we must not identify ourselves with those parts. If you believe in the problem of another, you are believing in something outside the self. You will best help others by realising the oneness of everything rather than by outward activity.

Desire - You are always pure. It is your senses and body which tempt you and which you confuse with your real self. So first know who is tempted and who is there to tempt. But even if you do commit adultery, don't think about it afterwards, because you are yourself always pure. You are not the sinner. The self is reached by the search for the origin of the Ego and by diving into the heart. This is the direct method of self-realisation. One who adopts it need not worry about channels, the brain centre, kundalini, Sushumna or chakras.

Yoga means union, it is really nothing but ceasing to think that you are different from the self or reality. The power that created you has created the world as well. If it can take care of you, it can similarly take care of the world also. *Samadhi* - Awareness of the self. The state in which the unbroken experience of existence consciousness is attained by the still mind.

Are you in the world or is the world within you? The world is your thought and your creation and projections. The world is real when it is experienced as the self and unreal when it is seen as separate names and forms. There is neither past nor future. There is only present. Yesterday was the present to you when you experienced it, and tomorrow will be also the present when you experience it. Therefore, experience takes place only in the present and beyond experience, nothing exists. If you are not the body and you have no birth and death. It is you who think that you will be reborn. Know yourself before you seek to decide about the nature of God and the world. I Am That I Am is the absolute being is what is. It is the self, it is God. Knowing the self, God is known. The bliss of self is always it's you and you will find it for yourself if you would seek it earnestly. The cause of your misery is not in the lie outside you, it is you as the Ego. Creation is neither good nor bad, it is as it is. A woman is a woman, but one mind calls her mother, another sister, and another aunt, and so on. These value judgements are the cause of all the misery in the world.

Creation is like a peepul tree; Birds come to eat its fruit or take shelter under its branches, humans cool themselves in its shade, but some may hang themselves on it. Yet the tree continues to lead its quiet life, unconcerned with and unaware of all the uses it is put to. In creation, there is room for everything, but human refuses to see the good, the healthy and the beautiful. He who thinks he is the doer is also the sufferer. The idea of good in the heart is enough. Good, God, love are all the same things. If an individual keeps continuously thinking of any one of these, it will be enough. There never was and never will be a time when all are equally happy or rich or wise or healthy. In fact, none of these terms has any meaning except in so far as the opposite to it exists. You must love all and help all, since only in that way can you help yourself.

Peace is the absence of disturbance. The disturbance is due to the arising of thoughts in the individual, which is only the Ego rising from pure consciousness. To bring world peace means to be free from thoughts and to abide by pure consciousness. If one remains at peace oneself, there is only peace everywhere. Bad habits and bad conduct are like a wound in the body. Every disease must be given appropriate treatment. If one knows the truth that all that one gives to others is giving only to oneself. Everyone is one's own self, whoever does whatever to whoever is doing it only to him/herself. Public speeches, physical activity and material help are all outweighed by the silence of great souls or people of wisdom.

Your eyes cannot see themselves. Place a mirror before them and they see themselves similarly with creation. See yourself first and then see the world as the SELF.

In silence we speak, in silence we see our truest selves, in this social media age of constant gratifications, validations, distractions, notifications, silence has become a precious commodity. Silence allows us to focus on inner calm and helps us connect with our True Self. In silence, we find truth and become connected with our True Self

Ancient Greek and roman philosophers frequently regarded noise as a serious distraction, one that challenged their ability to concentrate. One example is philosopher Seneca described in great detail the noises coming from a bathhouse just below the room where he was writing, expressing his irritation at the distraction all around him. At the end he has decided to withdraw to the countryside for quietness and peace.

The visionary scientists like Albert Einstein and Isaac Newton worked almost exclusively alone for majority of their lives. The best creative work is often completed in solitude or after a period of solitude. When we look into the history, the best creative work by painters, artists, poets, scientists and other creative minds happened when their outside world is shut out and purely focused on their craft.

Language is only a medium for communicating one's thoughts to another. It is called in only after thoughts arise. 'I' thought is the root of all conversation. Most advanced seeker in Silence is ever speaking, and others require words to explain the truth, but the truth is beyond words. It doesn't admit of explanation.

Speech is at best an honest lie. While silence is at worst a naked truth. In silence there is clarity, in noise there is confusion. In stillness there is calm, in excess motion there is excess nervous energy. We all love music, but music is the space and silence between the notes. The music is not in the notes, but in the silence between. The beauty needs a certain amount of emptiness and silence to be appreciated. The silence between the notes allows them to resonate and reach their full measure of expression.

The same applies to our lives, too much clutter can limit our creativity and make our lives chaotic. If life milestones are the music notes, then the time between the milestones are the silences. Finding moments of silence can have significant advantages both on psychological and mental wellbeing, with all of the constant noise we hear on a day to day basis, embracing silence can help to concentrate and process all things. Silence is an important part of the creative process and from spiritual aspect awareness is achieved through silence.

In today's hyper connected world being busy is a badge of honour, and we are all addicted to that being busy and complain about not having free time, yet we spend hours on social media or binge watching some shows. Being busy is overrated, and what it does is instead of taking time to pause, reflect on appreciating beautiful moments, we jump into taking another task.

One simple thing we all can do to achieve silence, is simply being in the nature. In nature silence is loud. The best way to experience divine is through the silence. A quote from Mother Teresa, we need to find God and he cannot be found in noise and restlessness. God is the friend of silence. See how nature, trees, flowers, grass grows in silence, see the stars, the moon and the sun, how they move in silence, we need silence to be able to touch souls.

Personally, I spend lot of time in nature, almost every day I spend time looking at the sunrise and sunset in silence. At times I have tears of joy simply looking at the nature and being in the nature. Calming, peaceful and pleasant experience. So, what did silence teach me?

Silence taught me to be happy with less. Silence taught me that a few simple words well-spoken have more power than hours of chatter.

Silence taught me to appreciate the value of listening. Deep listening expresses deep appreciation.

Silence taught me to take time each day to notice my thoughts and let go of the thoughts that don't serve me.

Silence taught me to notice nature & the rich texture of sounds it offer. By taking a short walk in nature in silence, I discover the pleasantness and peace that nature has to offer.

Silence taught me to feel my body and how it can calm my troubled mind and to open my heart. Silence taught me that space helps me face hard times. The times to face something difficult, pause and reflect.

Silence taught me that love can be simple. Think of someone you haven't said I love you to recently and tell them. Silence reminded me that speaking is easy, but staying quiet is hard. Silence taught me the importance of telling the truth.

Silence has taught me a deeper truth than words ever could.

At the start and end of every day I sit in silence and ask myself what I am grateful for. Sit in silence once a week and feel the truth in your heart. It's there whether you can express it in words or not.

Silence can be your best friend who never betrays, listen to the silence beyond the words and you shall hear the divine tune. This silence and space can be achieved with exercise, yoga, meditation, walk in woods, swimming, bike ride or simply being in nature alone.

I hope you will find some alone activity, which gives you the space and silence.

CHAPTER FIVE

Witnessing

A witness to both life and death

On the 19th of November 2020, I received an urgent call from my family in India. My father had been admitted to intensive care and was in critical condition. His kidneys were failing, and his heart no longer functioned properly, leading to anaemia. Given his history of cancer, chemotherapy, paralysis and kidney disease, the outlook was grim. I had to be by his side.

International travel in the middle of the coronavirus pandemic was a frustrating, and often surreal experience. Though I gained an exemption from the Australian government allowing me to leave, that was only the beginning. There were many state and airline-imposed COVID-safe processes to work through, new rules and regulations that changed from country to country, and a chaotic sea of confused, anxious travellers. Usually, people are in good spirits when they travel, but the passengers I observed during this time seemed sad – something I could sense from behind their face masks. Throughout the journey, in airports and on planes, I felt a pervading sense of tension.

In the midst of all this activity, I kept myself calm, at peace with my silence. I took the role of a witness – watching my own mind and body, drawing on what I had learned over the years in my quest for truth. I had been longing to visit the Ramana Maharshi ashram for a while, and deep inside I felt that my journey to India was not only to care for my father, but it was also in reply to this longing.

Finally, I reached Chennai and drove to Nellore, where my father was hospitalised. There were many more COVID protocols to get through to be allowed to visit and stay with him in his private room. Grateful to have made it to his bedside, nothing scared or bothered me as I began caring for him. I sat with him as he slept or endured dialysis which could last for hours. I helped him to the toilet, massaged his aching muscles, and administered what medicine he needed. Sometimes, the best thing I could do was simply to talk to him, to be present. Everything happens for a reason, and my purpose at that point was to be by his side. It reminded me, in a way, of the serious health issues I had recently faced.

I knew that we were borrowing time for my father, keeping him alive for maybe a few months more. His body fought to keep going, but his eyes told a different story, one of a man coming closer and closer to death. At night looking into his eyes seemed like looking into the innocent eyes of a child.

Many times, as I cared for him, my father asked, 'why is this happening to me?' Drawing on the wisdom I had gained over a lifetime of searching, I did my best to answer. With humility, I explained what I had learned about the cycle of life and death, about karma, and the difference between the true self, the mind and the body. I don't know how much I was able to get through to him. We have always had different mindsets and saw the world in very different ways. From his hospital bed, he questioned my belief that everyone is equal and should be treated as such, arguing that I would fail if I approached life in this way. His short-sighted views perplexed me, though I understood they were generated by primitive human survival instincts and his life experience. Knowing that I would never change his mind, I let the argument rest so he could be at peace. After all, his health was critical, and who was I to judge him?

Every night he edged closer to death, but every morning he opened his eyes, and in this, I saw the cycle of life and death unfurl around me.

While in India attending to my father, I could also oversee the completion of a temple to our local goddess, named after the river Ganges. For the past decade, our village had been trying to have a temple built but needed support to see it progress. The last time I visited India, in 2019, my father promised that our family would aid in its construction. I saw this as a wonderful opportunity to get involved for the good of the community.

There are many ceremonies involved in the completion of a temple. Until this point, our goddess had been worshipped in the form of three stones that were infused with her energy. The most recent had been installed twenty years ago, the one before that fifty years ago, but the oldest of the stones had been there for at least two hundred years, and was possibly up to five hundred years old, dating back to the time of kings and queens. Throughout January we had a temporary, wooden effigy, while the new temple and its idol were completed. The first ceremony, held in December, was to dig up the stones and relocate them, burying them in the site marked for the new statue. Over the next month, the energy of the goddess was imbued into the statue, culminating in its ritual immersion in the Bay of Bengal. In early January, the temple was officially opened. This was a time for great celebration, held over two days of ceremony and prayer. Seven priests were present, and the temple, the goddess and the entire community decked in colourful garlands of five different flowers and five different kinds of fruit, to represent the five elements of earth, water, air, space and fire.

As the eldest son in my family, I was at the centre of it all. Officially, my role began in January, with the opening of the temple. Even before then, I oversaw as much of the progression as possible, including carrying the wooden effigy as it was immersed, and the final statue when it was invested. The project was my father's dream, his legacy, and I was happy to see it happen. I did my best to represent him, as he was not well enough to attend.

However, the temple became another source of conflict between us. My father grew upset that I was doing this work without him and accused me of returning to India not to care for him, but to advance my own importance in the village. It felt like a moment of truth between us, where the resentment he had harboured for so long finally came to a head. He despised my independence, and how I'd rejected the plans he'd made for my life. We had suddenly gone back in time, to the way things were twenty years ago when I left my family and moved to Sydney. His health was failing, but he still attempted to pressure me into marrying an Indian girl and staying in the country, conspiring with other family members behind my back. I had come to India with the purest intentions, but because of this increasing conflict, I decided it was time to return to Australia. To close that chapter and continue with my own simple, pleasant life.

This was not a decision I made thoughtlessly, and saying goodbye to my father was hard. I touched his hand and looked into his eyes, searching for a connection deeper than words. Though our vision of the world and attitude towards life had never aligned, I hoped he could see me for who I truly am. His eyes, soft with tears and vulnerability, would be the last image I captured. A strong, stubborn personality who had suddenly become a helpless child. In my heart, I asked him to forgive me for never being the son he wanted me to be. Ramana Maharshi's analogy of the cinema screen came to mind. In this analogy, the movie is our mind and emotion, but the screen it is projected on is the true self. I could only hope at that moment that my screen would not be overwhelmed by what was in front of me.

A journey from India to Sydney with the pandemic still raging was going to be a long one and involve transfers at Dubai and Colombo. Fifty-five hours in transit, and fourteen days quarantine once I arrived. Even so, I embarked on it but had only made it as far as Dubai when I received a call to say my father's condition had worsened. He didn't have much time left. Unsure whether I was making the right choice, I tried to cancel my trip and book a flight back to Chennai. The universe was testing me, and I believed I had a responsibility to return. But something deep inside me didn't want to go back. Perhaps I simply had nothing left to give to India.

As it turned out, returning was not a simple thing to do, and my plans were constantly disrupted by COVID regulations and unreliable flights. The whole time I kept reminding myself to act only as a witness, and that life would take me where I needed to be. If I was meant to go back to Sydney, then I would find a flight. If I needed to be in India, then that's the flight I would take. But lack of sleep is deadly, and as the hours and days dragged by, as flight after flight was cancelled, as I spent countless stretches of time trying to rest in chaotic airport lounges, I began to lose my sense of self and purpose. Where was the right place for me?

During this time, I found strength in the teachings of the philosopher J. Krishnamurti. Looking beyond the five senses, he says that life is nothing but energy and that we can channel this energy to have a greater impact on the physical world. Observing the observer is what allows us inward access to true consciousness. Reality is when time and thought stop, meaning the experiencer doesn't experience anything. While we all chase and seek experiences, only nothingness is real.

After many days in transit and very little sleep, I returned to India, carrying a boarding pass that said, *Place of origin: Chennai – Destination: Chennai*.

I endured December and January on a physical, emotional, and financial rollercoaster. I had bruises on my left shoulder from carrying my father, helping him move from bed to chair, chair to bed, countless times every night. I had bruises on my right shoulder from carrying the statue of the goddess as part of the ceremonies to open the temple. It all had left me battered, drained and exhausted.

On the 17th of January 2021, my father passed away. The day before, as his brain and body began to shut down, I had decided to cease medical intervention. He wanted no more tubes in his nose or needles in his veins. I was at his bedside, holding his hand as he took his last breath, and felt a mixed sense of sadness and relief. Afterwards, I travelled in an ambulance to take his body home, as I had with my mother back in 2004.

The loss of my father produced a complicated form of grief in me. Ours was always a difficult relationship, and though it continued that way right to his death, I wish him a peaceful journey. As the eldest son, I performed his funeral rites in accordance with Indian tradition. Every night, I fasted. Every morning, I made an offering for his soul: breaking a coconut, lighting lamps, and feeding crows. In Hindu culture, crows are believed to be our ancestors, returned to earth. By offering the birds Shradh food, we honour those we have lost.

On the 4th of February, I invited almost two hundred and fifty people to attend the final prayers for my father. On this day, known as the Big Karma Day, I led devotions to help his soul pass from this life to the next. The main part of the day is the Hindu tradition of offering Pinda to recently departed souls, to unite them with their ancestors. *Pindas* are balls of cooked rice and flour mixed with black sesame seeds. The first rice ball is offered to my father, the second to my grandfather, and the third to my great grandfather. They are also offered to the crows. My final duty was to sleep in a temple. I travelled an hour to the Srikalahasti temple (Sri meaning spider, Kala meaning snake, and Hasti meaning elephant). The temple represents air, one of the five elements in the name of Lord Shiva. Sleeping at the temple allows for any negative energies I was carrying to be left there.

The next day, I managed to escape the village and finally visit the Ramana Maharishi ashram. It is in Tiruvannamalai, an area rich with history and nestled in the Annamalai foothills, which was ruled by kings from the 9th century until the arrival of the British. The city is 200 kms from my village in south India and the place is of high spiritual significance for south Indians. The city has a legend, Goddess Parvati, wife of lord Shiva, once closed the eyes of her husband playfully in a flower garden at their abode atop Mount Kailash near Himalayas. Although only a moment for the gods, all light was taken from the universe, and the earth, in turn, was submerged in darkness for years. Parvati performed penance with other devotees of Lord Shiva, and her husband appeared as a big column of fire at the top of Annamalai hills, returning light to the world. He then merged with Parvati to form half-female; half-male body equally split in the middle. This body form represents the synthesis of masculine and feminine energies of the universe and illustrates how energy, the female principle of God, is inseparable from the male principle of God, and vice versa. People travel to this spiritual place to find light, when going through darkness in life. Also reminds us we are all made of equal energy of feminine and masculine. On the day I arrived, the town was bursting with happy, smiling locals, performing a ceremony to worship a local goddess. Relaxing chants woke me the next morning, echoing down streets full of wandering peacocks. That day I climbed the Arunachala hills and visited the cave where Ramana Maharishi meditated. Virupaksha was Ramana Maharishi's guru, a saint from the 13th century. He spent most of his life in this cave and chose to be buried alive there. Afterwards, I visited a 9th-century temple dedicated to Lord Shiva, and finally the Ramana Maharishi ashram. I spent time meditating in the ashram, feeling Ramana Maharishi's energy, reflecting on his teachings and the knowledge I have gained.

That evening, I took a long walk 14 kilometres around a hill called Girivalam, to reflect on the last moments I spent with my father, and what I had gone through during this visit to India. Built on this hill is an octagonal structure, signifying the eight Lingams.

Lingams are an ancient representation of the first form and divine energy of the Hindu deity Shiva, a symbol of the supreme consciousness and cosmos. The eight Lingams represent Indra (Heaven), Agni (Fire), Yama (Death), Niruthi (Demons), Varuna (Rain, Water), Vayu (Wind), Kubera (Wealth) and Esanya (Peace, Contentment). I noticed many sadhus (holy men who have given up all worldly possessions) and passed massive Banyan trees that could have been two to five hundred years old. Banyan trees are mentioned in ancient Indian texts and scriptures and represent the divine creator. They symbolise longevity and immortality.

During my time in India, caring for my father at the end of his life, I became a witness to many things. With patience and silence, I observed the thin line between life and death. It was a constant reminder to appreciate this precious life, and not to waste it on petty, egotistical selfishness. This feels like a natural extension of my journey of self-enquiry, a witnessing I had anticipated would come from my next trip to India. These were not the circumstances that I had imagined, but as always, I allow the truth to come to me in a natural, organic way. Life goes on, and I wish my father peace in his passing because death is not the end of our journey. Being a witness in India to my father's ill health and death, as well as the construction and opening of the temple, felt to me like a river reaching the ocean, and its final resting place.

With my father and mothers' death, I understood the power of acceptance. Yes, acceptance is a choice but a hard choice in life. We all face challenges in our lives, sometimes they are big ones, sometimes they are small. We all will struggle with them at some point in life. Life will bring many challenges, such as the death of someone we love, break up in relationships, critical health issues, and it is not easy to embrace them, when we are suffering and wishing those things would have never happened. But if we start cultivating acceptance in our lives, we will likely cope the future crisis in a different way and view them from a different perspective. We will start to accept instead of resisting.

The inability to accept change in your life can keep you stuck and keeps you drained.

In my own personal experience, the loss of my mother in year 2004 and my father in year 2021, had a different experience for me when it comes to acceptance. At the time, I hadn't seen my family for almost four years. No one had told me anything about my mother feeling unwell, or the many tests being done on a lump detected in her throat. When I saw her after 4 years, my mother had lost so much weight, she was only skin and bones. Tears in my eyes, speechless from shock, my entire world ground to a sudden halt. I felt none of the heat and humidity of Chennai, hardly even noticed the chaos and crowds of the city. All I saw, all I felt, all that mattered, was my mother. Slowly, my family revealed the truth to me. She had been diagnosed with throat cancer. The doctors told me that the cancer was in a late-stage, and she had less than six months to live. Heartbroken, I searched for answers and finally came across a doctor who was willing to operate. Despite all the efforts of the doctors, she passed away in 2004. I still remember taking my mother's body from Chennai to our village in south India for her burial rites. It was a four-hour journey. I remember holding her hand and touching her forehead, but all I could feel was the coldness of her skin. The reality that she was no longer in her body sunk into me with that feeling. Before my father's death in 2021, back in 2009, my father was diagnosed with mouth cancer. Luckily, it was diagnosed early, and with chemotherapy, he managed to survive. It took him a good twelve months from diagnosis to recovery.

But this is the nature of life; it presents us with unforeseen challenges, and it is up to us to make the most of every situation. I struggled to accept my mother's death and it took me almost a decade to accept her death. I had guilt and my grieving process was long. I felt I wasn't there for her, and I could have done something different, even though it wasn't in my control. Learning to accept my mother's death taught me to see my father's death differently.

I was more able to accept my father's death in 2021 better than I was able to with my mother's death. Acceptance of the truth and the reality in front of me, helped me to cope with my father's death.

What I realised is that the real beauty of life is that it is unpredictable. Nothing is permanent, everything changes, and lot of things can happen that will transform who I am and how those incidents have an impact on my life. The ability to truly accept whatever comes in life and able to embrace it, is not an easy process, but it can be done. Choose not to judge what happens to you, instead believe that everything happens for a reason and that the better things will always follow, that is the beginning of true acceptance.

Self-acceptance is an awareness of both positive and negative aspects of life. One practical way we can develop self-acceptance is through learning self-compassion. Many of us are harsh on ourselves than we are to others. Self-compassion is cultivating a kinder and more constructive inner voice towards us. Self-compassion and acceptance lead to happiness, optimism, life satisfaction, increased motivation, positive body image and taking care of health and us. Ikigai a Japanese purpose of life explains an adaptation and acceptance, no matter what the nature of that situation you might be. Ikigai and happiness come from the acceptance of the self, no matter what kind of unique features or circumstances one might happen to be born with. Acceptance is also divine. This deep divine state of acceptance is transformative and liberating. All-encompassing and all-inclusive; it doesn't discriminate.

The power of acceptance is, it leads to happiness, pleasantness and more peace with what had happened in our life and will prepare us on what other challenges life throws at us in future. No one is perfect, yet we often expect ourselves to be. When we learn to accept ourselves, we are likely to be happier and better at learning and growing. Acceptance is an active process and can be practiced. Acceptance is you are choosing to allow it to be there, when you can't change it in that moment. Making space for it, giving yourself permission to be as you are, feeling what you are feeling, or experiencing what you are experiencing without creating shame, anxiety or stress. Practicing acceptance prepares you to live in this changing world, where you never know what is going to happen next. Acceptance is like protecting yourself and taking care of yourself. We can practice acceptance towards our experience, people, appearance, emotions, ideas and literally in all areas of life.

We are all seeking joy and happiness in life, but *Why* Happiness has become a mirage in the modern world. Before we seek Joy and happiness, we need to understand the difference between Joy and happiness. Happiness is an emotion in which one experiences many feelings ranging from contentment, satisfaction to bliss and intense pleasure, whereas Joy is a stronger, less common feeling than happiness. Joy is a long-lasting state of being, whereas happiness can be short lived. Joy is something grander than happiness. Joy comes from our heart, and it is possible to experience Joy in difficult times. Joy can share space with other emotions like sadness, fear, anger, even unhappiness, but happiness can't share space with other emotions. Joy can be present where difficulties exist, but happiness can't live in this space. Joy and Sorrow go hand in hand - Your joy is your sorrow unmasked. They are inseparable the deeper that sorrow is carved into your being the more joy you can contain. The early Greek philosophers believed that happiness was a mental state all humans desired. However, happiness was achieved only by living with wisdom, justice and courage, seeking hedonistic pleasure was not true happiness. Joy is present in the moment and every moment. Happiness is temporary and its mostly passing through emotion. Joy is an inner feeling and endures hardships and connects with meaning and purpose.

Joy is constant while happiness is temporary. Joy is about selflessness while happiness involves pleasing oneself. Joy can be deeply spiritual while happiness lacks deep connection. Joy is meaningful while happiness feels good. Joy is a choice a person makes, while people chase after happiness. Joy is genuine connection with each other, while happiness consists of momentary connections. Joy is self-transformative while happiness can hold you back. Joy is a less common, stronger feeling than happiness.

If you are chasing for happiness, know that you will never be happy. Chasing happiness is like going after a mirage. Happiness is a mirage, the more you seek it, the farther away it gets.

A story about chasing the mirage of happiness, a traveller was on foot on a hot day. After a while, he became overcome by thirst and began following the mirage up ahead as if it were real. Quite by chance, his pursuit led him to a genuine riverbank flowing with fresh water. By this point, he is thirstier than ever. But without taking a single sip, he just stood there looking at the river. A bystander noticed the traveller on the riverbank and said, "you look incredibly thirsty, and yet you are standing here without taking a drink". The traveller replied, "I am so thirsty. But look at that river ahead. There is far too much water in there, how could I possibly finish it all?" The traveller became aware of a growing thirst within. His eyes locked on and chased the mirage of river up ahead. He followed his belief in the truth of this image. It looked real and he dedicated his journey to reaching it. It contained a promise. Water. Relief. Satisfaction. Refreshment. Mirages are always just a little further up the road. Looks like happiness, success, and that wholeness might shimmer like reachable and real places on the path ahead. Many of us lock eyes on them. And society often makes us to believe and chase these kinds of mirages. But when we get to where we thought we saw them, we usually find an empty space. The shimmering image is still on the horizon. Out of reach. Not because it is out of reach, but because it's not there at all. It's an illusion. A trick of the mind. In the story, the traveller has a stroke of luck and stumbles on a source of the very thing he thought was pursuing, which is the happiness. Yet he looks for more and the pursuit never ends. We create our own impossible mirages like the thirsty traveller, while chasing happiness. So, happiness is just like following Mirage. So seek for Joy and not just happiness. Happiness is important but if you are seeking for Joy, that can be attained and stay forever regardless of life challenges. Desire, comparison and greed are often the initiators of this pursuit of happiness often driven by our own ego.

A student asked his teacher, "What is Greed?" The teacher thought of explaining greed in a practical way, so she invited all students to the nearest chocolate factory. Once the students are at the factory, the teacher said, "In order to answer your question, go through the chocolate factory and pick the one chocolate you like the most. But there is a rule. As you pass through the factory, you cannot turn back. You must pick the chocolate as you go forward only." The student went to the chocolate factory. As he walked through, He saw the one chocolate wrapped nicely, he instantly liked it, but he wondered that he may find much bigger better one further. So, he walked further, then he saw another chocolate. But again, he thought the same, there might be something better. When he started to reach near the end of the factory, he couldn't see any chocolates as big, better as the one he didn't pick earlier and started to regret his decision of letting it go. Finally, he gave up. He went back to the teacher with an empty hand and explained what he did. The teacher told him, "You did like the one chocolate very much but still you kept looking for a bigger better one. And later you realized that what you let go off was the best chocolate you could find there. That my dear is called Greed."

We let go of many good things in our life because of our greed of having even better things. Our Human Nature is such that we always want better and better. But in the search of better, we let go of many good things which could have given us similar satisfaction and made us happy. Learn to make your choice wisely and have gratitude for what you have and learn to be in content. Once you are grateful and in contentment with your life, you will attain the peace and pleasantness in life. The peace and pleasantness you attain will have a ripple effect on others. This is the way you can have a greater positive impact towards the world.

Why is peace and pleasantness important, because everything we do in life, deep within us we are seeking and craving for peace and pleasantness, yet we struggle to find it. Enlightenment is nothing but achieving continuous peace and pleasantness in life, regardless of the life challenges and circumstances. Our true self is nothing but the peace and pleasantness, this state of being is our true nature. We struggle to attain peace and pleasantness because of worry. Worry comes from the unknown, and in our world today, so much is indeed without guarantee. Our world is unpredictable and dangerous, separations, loss and death are inevitable. All worry comes from fear, disappointment, or anything we deem as not being the way we want it to be. We worry about health, happiness, money, position, power, and status, acceptance, love, vulnerability, and insecurities. When worrying gets out of hand, it becomes anxiety and disturbs our peace. Persistent anxiety shows itself physically, through things such as fatigue, headache, bodily pain, sleep disturbances, and panic attacks. At its worst, such prolonged stress can cause heart attacks, strokes, and death.

Imagine a lake with calm waters with no ripples, that is peace and pleasantness doesn't matter the depth of the lake, once we throw a stone the ripples come. Thats what happens in our life, we get thrown at us many stones and we continue to feel the ripples and its consequences. Some stones are thrown by others and some by us. The bigger the stone, the bigger the ripple and the impact. Little things we do create ripple effects that can sometimes result in good things and sometimes make bad things happen to other people, even people we have never met. Suppose one morning you happen to see a friend who is grumpy and somewhat unhappy, and you give her a big smile and say hello. Since smiles are contagious, she gives you a smile right back and suddenly feels better. If so, she may smile at someone else. The ripple effect can continue to others, all from that one smile you gave.

A beautiful story about the ripple effect, One early evening on a lonely country road, an old man was standing on a bridge, high above a deep river. He had just dropped a pebble over the railing to see how long it would take to hit the water. As he watched the ripples fanning out, along came a pickup truck. It slowly came to a stop, but the motor was kept running. The old man noticed the name painted on the door: Florist delivering beautiful flowers - Live life in full bloom. Walking up to the window, he saw a man behind the wheel with his head bowed low, breathing heavily.

"Is anything wrong?" he asked. "Yes," the man said quietly, "I think I am having a heart attack. I am trying to get to the hospital." "Let me help you," said the old man. "You shouldn't be driving. The nearest hospital is a good 30 minutes from here." "I know," mumbled the man. "I'm John. I was all alone at my nursery, after my employees had left for the day." "Don't worry, John," said the old man. "I'll drive you there."

He opened the door, took the wheel, and drove as fast as he could down the road. When they arrived at the emergency entrance to the hospital, the attendants rushed out with a wheelchair and quickly wheeled John to the emergency room. The old man waited throughout the night. He knew what it was like to be all alone, without family or friends in times of need. He had lived alone since his wife had died several months before. The doctors were able to save John's life. They told the old man that John would have died if he had arrived just a few minutes later. A week passed. John was getting well. Several of his employees came to visit, as did the old man. While everyone was gathered around his bedside, John took the hand of the old man and said to his employees, "This dear and gentle man saved my life, though we were perfect strangers. And I want you to know, he created a ripple effect in all of our lives. By saving my life, he saved my business. By saving my business, he saved the jobs of thirty families. We all owe him so much." There was silence as all eyes turned toward the old man. He gave a gracious smile, but there were tears in his eyes. He gently leaned over the railing of the bed and whispered to John, "I must tell you something, John. You saved my life. Just about the time you drove up in your truck, I was about to jump off that bridge. Now I know how important every life on earth is to every other. It is just as you said, John, the ripple effect."

When a stone is thrown into the water, the ripple begins. We watch the splash. We see the ripple. We see the effect. But what happens as the rock travels below the water? Does it hit anything on the way down? What happens when it hits the bottom? What happens when we can't see the rock anymore? What happens under the surface? Choices are like rocks hitting the water. Choices have a ripple effect. With these choices, there is not only a ripple effect on the surface but also a sinking effect below the surface. As the choice settles on the bottom, it disrupts things blind to the naked eye. It disrupts deep down within our spirit and souls. Sometimes that disruption is good. Sometimes that disruption has horrifying consequences. The best way to achieve peace and pleasantness is by surrender, I surrendered to the pain growing up not seeing my parents, I surrendered to the pain caused in my relationships, I surrendered to the pain that I no longer had a grip on my parents death, I surrendered to the pain my inner child has gone through as a kid, I surrendered myself to the universe to simply guide me. All I know is that we each have a choice to do something about the season that we are in. When we are faced with an obstacle in front of us, we have the ability to put a stake in the ground, make a decision, and move forward. We all can create a new positive ripple effect to attend the peace we are seeking within. What does the water's rippling effect teach us? When water is disturbed, it accepts the disturbance. It does not complain, but fight against it, or try to grasp onto what it was before the disturbing, unwanted, or unexpected event. Water does not have any expectations about life, what it should be and what it's existence or work will produce. Water just is. It has no attachments, has no illusions of its value, and demands nothing. Water relinquishes control simply because it's its nature, just like our true nature. And in doing these things or being this way, water overcomes the need to worry. When water ripples then, the lessons it teaches us that life goes on despite what we do or don't do. What has occurred is already past, so let it go and accept the learning embedded in it. Let go of worry and anxiety. Focus on the now, the current flow. Choose to control only on that which is controllable, that is, ourselves, our minds, our hearts, and our responses of acceptance, flow, and settle. When we do this, we are being proactive rather than reactive and can operate from a place of peace rather than from stress.

When you feel fear in life remind yourself of the river and the fear poem by Khalil Gibran.

It is said that before entering the sea, a river trembles with fear.

She looks back at the path she has travelled, from the peaks of the mountains, the long winding road crossing forests and villages. And in front of her, she sees an ocean so vast, that to enter there seems nothing more than to disappear forever. But there is no other way. The river cannot go back. Nobody can go back. To go back is impossible in existence. The river needs to take the risk of entering the ocean, because only then will fear disappear, because that's where the river will know, it's not about disappearing into the ocean, but of becoming the ocean.

Fear of failure is one of the main reasons we give up in life. The same fear that is attempting to protect us from disappointment is hampering our ability to succeed. Majority people give up as they expect fast results, stop believing in themselves, get stuck in the past, dwell on mistakes, fear the future, resist change, give up their power, believe in their weaknesses, feel the world owes them something, fear of failure more than desire success, never visualise what is possible, feel they have something to lose, overwork, assume their problems are unique, see failure as the signal to turn back and feel sorry for themselves. A bamboo and fern story about patience and persistence, when you feel like giving up in life. When you feel like quitting or giving up, remember this fern and the bamboo story. A student has decided to quit everything he was practicing & was frustrated with life itself. He was feeling lost and defeated. He had tried so hard to succeed, but it seemed like everything he did was a failure. He was ready to give up. Feeling defeated with life, he went to see his Master & shared his disappointment. The master said, I understand your disappointment and why don't we go for a walk in nature and discuss. The student agreed and while both the master and student started walking in the nature close to where the master lived, Master showed the student two plants and asked, "Do you see the two plants there? The fern and the Chinese bamboo?" The student nodded yes. The Master continued, pointing towards two plants. "I planted both the fern & the bamboo seeds; I took very good care of them with water & sunlight".

Within a short period of time the fern quickly grew from the earth, but despite the Bamboo seed being watered and nurtured for a year, nothing came from the bamboo seed. In the second year the fern grew more vibrant and plentiful. But nothing came from the bamboo seed. In the third year, there was still nothing from the bamboo seed. Patience is tested and it almost feels like giving up. In the fourth year, there was nothing from the bamboo seed. Again, the patience is tested, and we begin to wonder if our efforts will ever be rewarded. Then in the fifth year a tiny sprout emerged from the earth. But six months later the bamboo grew to over 100 feet tall. "Just like the bamboo, know that the time you are struggling, you are growing foundation of strong roots", said the Master. Also, the higher you grow, the deeper you bow. It teaches gratitude and humility.

The bamboo story teaches patience, persistence, faith, growth and that every person has potential. The bamboo story asks you to have faith in your potential and one day, your hard work and persistence will finally make you fulfil your dreams. Don't compare yourself to others. Everyone has their own journey and their own pace. Just focus on your own growth and don't worry about what others are doing. Be patient & trust the process. It takes time to grow strong roots. Don't give up on your dreams just because you don't see results immediately. The bamboo tree's ability to bend without breaking teaches us the importance of flexibility in life. Instead of resisting change or challenges, we should adapt and bend when necessary to overcome obstacles. Despite being bent under pressure, the bamboo tree remains firmly rooted in the ground. This resilience reminds us to stay strong and grounded during tough times, knowing that we have the inner strength to withstand adversity. When faced with difficulties, the bamboo tree bows down but doesn't break. This humility teaches us the importance of being humble and open-minded, especially when facing challenges beyond our control. Just as the bamboo tree turns stress into its strength, we too can transform challenges into opportunities for growth. By embracing difficulties and learning from them, we can emerge stronger and more resilient individuals. Overall, the story of the bamboo tree inspires us to cultivate flexibility, resilience, humility, and the ability to turn adversity into strength in our own lives.

The story of the bamboo and the fern is a constant reminder that we should never give up on our dreams, no matter how difficult things may seem. The bamboo may grow slowly, but it eventually grows taller than the fern. This is a metaphor for how we should be patient and persistent in our efforts to achieve our goals. We should also not compare ourselves to others. Everyone has their own journey and their own pace. Focus on becoming your best version and don't worry about what others are doing.

Never give up on your dreams. You must never give up & sometimes shake off your problems, just like the donkey. A man's favourite donkey falls into a deep pit. He can't pull it out no matter how hard he tries. He therefore decides to bury it alive. Soil is poured onto the donkey from above. The donkey feels the load, shakes it off, and steps on it. More soil is poured. It shakes it off and steps up. The more the load was poured, the higher it rose. By noon, the donkey was grazing in green pastures. After much shaking off problems & stepping up learning from them, one will graze in green pastures. Overcome the problems instead of giving up & getting buried alive.

In the process of pursuing and achieving your dreams, you will face not just fear but also pain. By understanding the purpose of pain, you will break through the pain, just like the lotus must grow in the mud. Why it is important for us to break through the pain. Pain is inevitable, and beyond pain lies an eternal fact, that we are all unconditionally vulnerable. Doesn't matter who we are, rich, poor, good, bad, healthy, unhealthy, male, female, tall, short, big, small, white, black, brown, we will all go through various types of pain from our childhood to adulthood and to old age. No one can escape from pain; it is a universal language which takes us into unknown emotional depths and onto a journey into deep waters. It is the most powerful and intense experience we all must face in our lifetimes. Pain is unfiltered and raw, takes you down to the core of your true bring. It stabs you deep, but you are not broken. When we perceive pain or fall into its depths as a weakness, then we lose all power to grow and wisdom it teaches us. Running away or trying to escape from pain, is like running away from ourselves. We can't avoid pain, as it binds us as one humanity and is part of our existence. We cannot hate what really hurts us, because that only causes more pain and hurt to us. Instead of hurting ourselves more, we can choose first to accept that pain is inevitable and by understanding the pain, we can go through a process and eventually break through the pain. In this process which may seem going against our own will but comes wisdom. Thats one of the main purposes of pain, to gain wisdom and growth. We live in a superficial world, where being positive is seen as success and supreme. Expressing pain is seen as weakness and failure. We fear pain because it highlights to us just how fragile and exposed, we truly are. We need to understand that pain do not distinguish between the brave and fearful, the rich and the poor, or the loved and the lonely. We fear to express pain, so we try our best to sink it or disguise it from others.

We hide and disguise our pain, when all it truly wants is to be seen, heard, understood and accepted. In the process of hiding our grief and pain, we hurt ourselves and pass the hurt onto others that we care. It becomes a cycle of pain and sorrow, until we are strong enough to break the cycle by accepting and understanding pain. We hide our inner grief and pain beneath a fake smile or fake happiness. But our eyes are the windows to our soul, and they always speak the truth. The purpose of pain can be related to a lotus flower growing out of mud, darkness and water. At first the lotus seed is in complete darkness under water in mud. For a seed to achieve its greatest expression, it must transform by breaking its own shell in the darkness and the mud, it must come out and then everything changes. Think of pain as the seed, the mud and the water. The seed represents our capacity to transform not only our pain but also the suffering of others. The mud represents the darker side within us. All the troublesome, painful thought and emotions that afflict us on a day-to-day basis, like anger, desire, jealousy, ego and pride. The lake or water represents the depths of your existence, while the surface of the lake is the boundary between your unconscious and conscious thoughts and desires. The lotus seed makes the lotus flower shoot from seed to sprout. the shoot continues to grow until it breaks the surface of the water. Even though lotus is grown out of the mud, once it blooms and breaks the surface of the water, the lotus flower is entirely unmarked by the mud. The most crucial part of the lotus story is that the lotus flower cannot exist without the mud as the mud was the actual manure that fed the plant and made it. So, it is not about running away from the pain within yourself, Instead, it's about acknowledging painful feelings and seeing them as a potential source of self-transformation.

Our task through the darkest of times is to find a way to swim through the murky waters of hurt, sorrow, mental and emotional pain and come out the other side, stronger and more beautiful. Just like the lotus flower, we can elevate and rise through the shadows and darkness. A rebirth within you. Once you break through your pain. You are like the beautiful and colourful lotus, elevating through the darkest depths to stand taller and stronger, facing the sun with elegance. The main purpose of pain is growth. The lotus flower is an example of self-transformation and self-growth, breaking through the darkness within us. The lotus flower is a symbol that brings hope and growth. Likewise, as the flower rises above the mud, although it might seem impossible, so too we can rise above pain and suffering. A lotus flower is born in muddy water, grows in muddy water and rises out of muddy water to stand above it untouched by mud, we are also born in the muddy world, raised in the muddy world, having to overcome the muddy world, and still be able to live untouched by the muddy people and the muddy world. Next time think about lotus when you are going through pain or suffering. Rise from the dark muddy waters and transform that pain into progress to reach your potential. Once you transform the pain into kindness, compassion and love, you will receive all the beautiful things in life. Kindness and compassion are the bridge between pain and love. Where there is love, there is also wealth and success. Love acts as a magnet and attracts joy and happiness. Wealth, often misconceived as mere affluence, reveals its true nature when entwined with Love a richness that transcends material abundance, encompassing joy, fulfillment, and generosity. Success, the elusive pursuit of many, finds its zenith when harmonized with Love. True success is not measured by accolades alone but by kindness, empathy, and compassion left on the tapestry of humanity.

The convergence of Wealth and Success with Love is not mere coincidence, but a universal truth unveiled. In embracing

Love, we embrace a state of being that attracts abundance in its myriad forms. The resonance of this truth reverberates through the cosmos and is our being.

The parable of three old men is the choices we make in our lives. It prompts us to evaluate our priorities, urging us to discern the essence of true abundance.

A woman came out of her house and saw three old men with long white beards sitting in her front yard. She did not recognize them. She said, "I don't think I know you, but you must be hungry. Please come in and have something to eat." "Is the man of the house home?" they asked. "No", she said. "He's out." "Then we cannot come in", they replied. In the evening when her husband came home, she told him what had happened. "Go tell them I am home and invite them in," her husband said. The woman went out and invited the men in. "We do not go into a house together," they replied. "Why is that?" she wanted to know.

One of the old men explained: "His name is Wealth," he said pointing to one of his friends, and said pointing to another one, "He is Success, and I am Love." Then he added, "Now go in and discuss with your husband which one of us you want in your home." The woman went in and told her husband what was said. Her husband was overjoyed. "How nice!" he said. "Since that is the case, let us invite Wealth. Let him come and fill our home with wealth!" His wife disagreed. "My dear, why don't we invite Success?" Their daughter was listening from the other corner of the house. She jumped in with her own suggestion: "Would it not be better to invite Love? Our home will then be filled with love!" After a deep conversation between themselves, husband said to his wife. "Let us heed our daughter's advice," Please go out and invite Love to be our guest. The woman went out and asked the three old men, "Which one of you is Love? Please come in and be our guest." Love got up and started walking toward the house. The other two also got up and followed him. Surprised, the lady asked Wealth and Success: "I only invited Love, why are you coming in?" The old men replied together: "If you had invited Wealth or Success, the other two of us would've stayed out, but since you invited Love, wherever He goes, we go with him. Wherever there is Love, there is also Wealth and Success!"

In the pursuit of success, wealth and happiness, we first need clarity in life. How to find clarity over confusion. In our increasingly complex world, we often encounter many challenges that can leave us feeling overwhelmed, dis-empowered, confused & conflicted. Many of the things that concern us today are clearly beyond our control, yet we cannot seem to stop worrying about them. However, worrying about what we cannot control is not a wise use of our energy.

Confusion is a state of being where you feel unsure about what to do, what actions to take, a big uncertainty about what is happening, intended, or required. Confusion is the quality or state of being unclear. Confusion is created by our monkey minds, it is the feeling of to-do list that's created in your mind when you have all kinds of conflicting thoughts, for example, do it, don't do it, take a chance, why fix what's not broken and so on. You seriously entertain or you innocently treat those thoughts as if they are each deserving of consideration. Real as it seems, the confusion is an illusion of mind. You always know what you want to do deep within, but you have too much thinking about it all, instead of going with what you feel deep down. You have a lot more clarity than you think. So how to make decisions from a state of confusion, it can be achieved by understanding the circles of Influence, Concern and Control.

The ancient philosophers held that we could live more peaceful and fulfilling lives, if we focus our attention and energy on what we can control. Spending our mental energy wisely is of great importance, especially for those of us who are prone to anxiety, worrying, over thinking & exhausted. The ancient philosophers agreed that within our control are our thoughts, emotions, and interpretations, as well as our reactions and actions. These are the things that we should focus on and work to improve. By contrast, they held that there are things that are clearly outside of our control. These include other people's actions, feelings, and opinions of us, the weather, the economy, and random events in life. These are the things that we should not waste our energy worrying about. The circle of control can be a difficult concept to grasp, especially in a world where we often feel like we need to be in control of everything. However, accepting the idea that there are some things that we simply cannot control can be profoundly liberating. It can help us let go of anxiety, stress and focus on the things that we can change.

The first and smallest circle is the circle of control, representing aspects of our life over which we have direct control. The circle of control symbolizes the areas where we can take meaningful action and make a positive difference. This area focuses on our inner lives: our thoughts, beliefs, emotions, interpretations, and judgments of external events. We should try to focus most of our attention, energy, and resources on this region.

The second, slightly larger circle is the circle of influence, representing the intersection of factors within our immediate control and those that fall outside of our control. This is, quite literally, a grey zone. We may or may not have the power to expand our influence into this region to create change. We can certainly try. It is wise to spend some of our energy in that sphere, bearing in mind that we can control our efforts in this sphere, but not necessarily outcomes.

The third and largest, outermost circle represents the circle of concern. This circle focuses on a broader range of external factors, challenges, and circumstances that we may care about, but which are clearly beyond our control. This circle includes the economy, climate, weather, world peace, threat of war, government policy, death, where you are born, traffic, economy, others behaviours, social media comments, celebrities behaviours, media, sport match, public transport being on time, past decisions, past choices, and past behaviours, but also most of the actions, reactions, behaviours, and feelings of other people. We cannot control the world around us, but we can control our reactions to it. By focusing on what we can control, we can develop a sense of inner calm and resilience that helps us to cope with the challenges of life. The circle of concern includes the events, situations, reactions, and phenomena that are clearly outside of our spheres of control and influence. To live full and rewarding lives, we need to learn to let go of trying to control anything that lives in this circle. This is of course much easier said than done. It involves the capacity to let go of our desire for control and, at the same time, to seek to control unhelpful ruminating. Once you get your thoughts in order, your mind feels less confused or conflicted leading to clarity. Your mind is the confusion voice, and your heart is the clarity voice. Your mind is the monkey mind, and your heart is the monk mind. The heart is a little more trustworthy, a little sounder, and a little more grounded. The mind is louder, more repetitive, and maybe even a little more passionate, but it lacks substance. So next time you feel confused, stuck or lost, think about the circles of control, influence and concern to reach from your confused mind to your heart, a state of peace and pleasantness.

Bear in mind in this process of clarity over confusion, no matter what you do, people will always judge you.

A man and woman were traveling with their donkey. First day, they passed through a town, both riding on his back. People whispered: "What a mean couple, putting all that weight on the donkey." Second day the man on the donkey & the woman walking beside. People whispered: "What a cruel man, forcing his partner to walk while he rides on the donkey." Third day the man walking & the woman on the donkey. People whispered: "What a careless man, letting his woman ride alone on the donkey." Fourth day both walking beside the donkey. People whispered: "What a stupid couple, why do they walk if they could ride on the donkey"

Just do what you feel right in your heart, & don't be distracted by judgements criticism. When you follow your heart, you are living a life of abundance and will start to unravel the purpose of life. You take the step, and the path appears. The biggest questions of life, what is our life purpose and meaning to our existence. How many times we ask ourselves, what is my life purpose and what is the reason for my existence. Most of the time we get answers depending on the age and stage of life. As a child, my purpose is having fun, playing, exploring, and learning. As in teens and early twenties, finding direction with my studies or work, building my social identity, and discovering my peers, friendships as essential purposes. When in adult life, we focus on family, career, status, and success as essential purposes. While depending on the age and stage of the life, we have many purposes, they may or may not connect with our life purpose. There's got to be more to life than, working from Monday to Friday and counting days to the weekend and waiting for salary to pay bills. We need to ask ourselves WHY 85 percent of working professionals are not happy with their work. The primary reason is lack of connection to the purpose and significance of one's work and life. Everybody has a life purpose, but many people remain unaware of it for their entire lives. The danger of being unaware of your life's purpose is that you may confuse it with your life goals, such as career, making money, and being successful. For many of us, Life purpose is derailed through our own cultural, social, and family conditioning. We are easily influenced and driven by the values and ideals that belong to our culture, society, and family, but are not our own. We need to fulfill those purposes to survive, succeed, and fit into culture, society, and family. But you also need to get clarity on the differences between the purposes you share, and the purpose that comes from the heart of your existence.

So how do we get clarity about life purpose. The purposes that shift according to your age and circumstances is not your life purpose. Life purpose is the unchanging part of you and the reason for your existence. Most cultures, religions and faiths across the world talk about this, The French call life purpose as raison d'etre meaning "reason for being" or "reason to be". The Greek philosophers called Eudaimonia meaning happiness, but the underlying message is about life purpose Knowing who you really are and understanding your unique potentials to live a purposeful life. The south Africans called it Ubuntu meaning interconnectedness and the essence of being human. It focuses on *I am because we are*. Understanding this philosophy can provide a powerful sense of purpose and deeper connection to what we do and why we do what we do. The Japanese call it *Ikigai* "meaning for life" or "what makes life worth living". In India, they call it *Dharma,* meaning "right way of living", and the "path of rightness" which explains life purpose in Hindu culture. It is the principle of good order which remains constant while change occurs, but dharma itself does not change. Dharma refers to your soul's purpose, the big reason why you are here. It is not just what you do, but how you do it, and WHY you do it. In China, they call it Daoism or Taoism philosophy, meaning *the way or path to life*, focuses on finding the purpose of life in the yin-yang symbol. *The Way* is to live spontaneously between order and chaos. Doesn't matter which culture, religion or faith, they all teach that the life purpose is the foundation of your life, the cohesion of your existence, your essence, and your being. Life purpose is not your passion, though passion may influence your life purpose. Much of life revolves around primal passions and instinct to survive, procreate and experience pleasures like food, sex, and other desires of life. Passion drives emotion and not the life purpose. Passions are many and ever-changing. They come and go with your needs, moods, and desires. Passion is the vehicle, not the destination. Also, your life purpose is not your ego. Ego can be so fragile and ever hungry for validation and attention. It takes a depth of self-knowledge, self-reflection, self-transformation, self-development, intelligence, and maturity to understand and stay away from distractions of your ego, such as, "I should be rich, famous, and beautiful". These ego-feeding distractions are steering you away from your life purpose. The majority of people never realize their life purpose because they are too busy trying to become products of their ego. Unfortunately, most will die not knowing their reason for existence. While your ego helps you to establish yourself in the world, it is also the enemy of life purpose. Our ego is the rope tied around us with boundaries and limitedness. A story about the elephant and the rope, explains we are conditioned to be bound rather than experience our full potential.

A tourist was passing by the elephants, he suddenly stopped, confused by the fact that these huge creatures were being held by only a small rope tied to their front leg. No chains, no cages. It was obvious that the elephants could, at any time, break away from the chains but for some reason, they did not. He saw a trainer nearby and asked why these animals just stood there and made no attempt to get away. "Well," trainer said, "when they are very young and much smaller, we use the same size rope to tie them and, at that age, it's enough to hold them. As they grow up, they are conditioned to believe they cannot break away. They believe the rope can still hold them, so they never try to break free." The man was amazed. These animals could at any time break free from their bonds but because they believed they couldn't, they were stuck right where they were. Like the elephants, human beings, as a child subconsciously absorb thoughts, emotions, behaviours and beliefs from your parents, society and environment. You automatically default to these conditioned beliefs and behaviours to interpret and respond to all your life experiences. Our parents shape our world, shape our thoughts and shape us. Our parent's bad habits become ours. Their conditioning behaviour also become ours. Humans go through life hanging onto a belief that we cannot do something, simply because we failed at it once before. Failure is part of learning; we should never give up in fear of failure. Those who break that conditioning or the rope of fear and failure will taste the freedom from the chains of society's expectations. The best way to understand life purpose is by understanding the concept of tree of life. The tree of life concept is simple and straightforward. It is a visual metaphor in which a tree represents your life and the various elements that make it up as past, present, and future. Whenever we look at a beautiful tree, the most essential parts of the trees are its roots; the trunk; and the crown. The Tree of Life teaches us three things from these three essential parts: connection, cultivation, & contribution. We connect with the roots; we cultivate the trunk & we contribute with the crown.

The roots are for self-development, the trunk for physical and emotional well-being, and the crown for contributions to others. When we talk about the roots, a healthy tree has healthy roots. The deeper the roots, the stronger the roots, the tree stands strong in storms, cyclones & hurricanes. The roots are not seen to our eyes. But the trunk & crown of the tree is visible to our eyes. Our achievements, materialistic things, money, accolades, charisma and our success are seen to people. What's not seen to the eyes of the people is our roots, our spiritual development, inner self and connection. If we do not work on what is unseen, it's very difficult to sustain what is seen. As the roots are unseen to the world. Deepen them by connection to the divine, spiritual practice by meditation and self-reflection. Strengthening the roots happens by connection. A deep Connection to our own selves, connection to nature & divine energy. The trunk of the tree is about cultivation of our emotional wellbeing, physical wellness and emotional stability. If your mind is restless, your emotional state is disturbed. And when your emotional state is disturbed, you are not living your full potential. your mind can make heaven out of hell or hell out of heaven. So, we need to cultivate the trunk to find our physical and emotional stability. The crown is about contribution. Giving back to community and society. The crown is our contribution to the world. The crown is where the fruits, leaves and the flowers come. And giving those fruits, flowers, leaves and the shade from the tree is your contribution to others. By bringing the concept of tree of life into your day-to-day life actions, you will be able to connect with your true self, cultivate your emotional and physical wellbeing and then able to contribute. In this process you will be able to find your life purpose and meaning to your existence. Every individual has a purpose and meaning to their existence, it is up to the individual to find the meaning to their being. In a world where many find themselves caught in the monotony of daily routines and short-term distractions, seeking for a deeper sense of purpose, it is reassuring to know that the quest to find purpose is readily available from a timeless ancient wisdom shared by different cultures across the ages.

All the answers you are seeking are within you, they reveal themselves as you take a closer look at your life experiences. The purpose and meaning of life start with knowing yourself, I mean the true self not your ego self. Know the value of your life and self-worth.

A story of father and son, father teaches son the value of life. One day the son goes to his father and says, 'What is the value of my life? His father gave him a stone and said son if you want to know the value of your life take this stone to the market. If someone asks for a price you can say nothing and raise two fingers. So, the boy did as his father told him and went off to the marketplace. Suddenly, an old woman appeared and asked her how much the stone was. The boy says nothing and just raises two fingers. Then the woman says two dollars? I'll take it. The son is shocked and runs back to his father. There was an old woman in the market, she wanted to give me two dollars for a stone.

Father says son, the next place I want you to go to the museum and if anyone asks for a price say nothing and raise two fingers. Immediately, son picks up the stone and goes to the museum. After a while there was a middle-aged man who asked the boy. How much does this stone cost? The boy says nothing and raises two fingers, and the man says 200 dollars.

Wow I'll take it. The boy was shocked and runs home to his father. A man in a museum wanted to buy a stone for 200 dollars.

Lastly, I want you to take the stone to a gemstone store. Go inside the store and if anyone asks for a price say nothing just raise two fingers. Then the son runs to a jewellery store. After finding it, he went inside and there was an old man at the counter. As the old man sees the stone he bounces and shouts oh my lord, he has a stone that he has been looking all my life. What do you want in exchange of this stone, how much does it cost? The boy says nothing and raises two fingers. And the old man says 20,000 dollars? I'll take it. The boy can't believe, and he rushed to his father. An old man at a jewellery store wanted to give me 20,000 dollars for a stone.

Do you learn now, the value of life? Life is about where you put yourself. You can choose if you want to be a 2 dollar stone or a 20,000 dollar stone. You may be a precious stone, even priceless, but people may value you based on their level of information, their belief in you, their motive, their ambition, and their risk-taking ability. But don't fear, you will surely find someone who will discern your true value. In the eyes of life, you are very precious. Respect yourself. You are Unique and no one can replace you. Don't undermine yourself. It doesn't matter where you came from, what colour your skin is, or even how much money you have. What matters is the place you choose to be in and who you surround yourself with. This story reminds us that there are people who go through a whole lifetime believing they are worth only two dollars, when in fact, they just surround themselves with people who see them as such. Within each person hides a diamond, and we choose to surround ourselves with people who see our worth and the diamond inside of us. We choose whether to pace ourselves in a marketplace or in a precious gem store. Choose the people who surround you wisely, it can make all the difference in your life.

It is up to you to determine the ***value of your life***.

ABOUT THE AUTHOR

Lokesh Babu was born in Nellore, South India in 1975, and educated at the University of Western Sydney. As the eldest son of a traditional Indian family, his life was scripted for him, and he was expected to follow the values and needs of the family. However, he defied expectations, began his own journey, and has embraced the best of eastern and western cultures. Lokesh now has a 15-year-old daughter from a previous relationship and lives with his current partner. He is a podcaster, frequent public speaker and liaison to corporates, industry groups and executives.

Before he completed 'The True Self', Lokesh faced many challenges in his life, including inequality, separation, the death of loved ones, illness, near bankruptcy, suicide and self-harm. His time in India during COVID pandemic, Lokesh while caring for his father at the end of his life, he became a witness to many things. With patience and silence, he observed the thin line between life and death. It was a constant reminder to appreciate this precious life, and not to waste it on petty, egotistical selfishness. For Lokesh it feels like a natural extension of his journey of self-enquiry.

The knowledge he gained through his research into ancient teachings, which forms the basis of The True Self, has helped him to overcome them and find joy within.

Connect with Loki

- Instagram @lokeshbabuofficial
- Facebook @lokesh.babu.official
- Threads @lokeshbabuofficial
- Tik Tok @lokeshbabuofficial
- YouTube @lokeshbabuofficial
- X Twitter @Lokeshbabuoffi
- LinkedIn @lokeshthondavada
- www.lokiofficial.com.au

BIBLIOGRAPHY

Swami Paramananda, "The Upanishads," Translation and commentary from the original Sanskrit text by Swami Pramananda, published by The Vedanta Centre, Boston Massachusetts USA, 1919.

Hume, Robert Ernest, "The Thirteen Principal Upanishads," Translated from the Sanskrit text with an outline of the philosophy of the Upanishads by Robert Ernest Hume, published by Humphrey Milford Oxford University Press, 1921.

"Sanatana Dharma," An elementary textbook of Hindu religion and ethics, Published by The Managing Committee Central Hindu College Benares Varanasi, 1916. Digitized for Microsoft Corporation from University of California Libraries.

Swami Satchidananda, "The Yoga Sutras of Patanjali," Translation and commentary from the Sanskrit text by Swami Satchidananda, published by Integral Yoga Publications, Virginia USA, first printing 1978.

"The Encyclopedia of Ancient History," Founded in 2009, Written and edited by an internationally diverse team of editors and contributors, online edition on Wiley online library. In 2021 renamed to "World History Encyclopedia."

de Botton, Alain, "The Consolations of Philosophy," First published by Hamish Hamilton, 2000, then published in Penguin Books 2001.

Daniel, David Mills, "Briefly: 25 Great Philosophers." Published by SCM press UK, 2011.

Tzu, Lao, "The Tao Te Ching," Translation by Stephen Addiss and Stanley Lombardo, Published by Hackett Publishing, 1993.

Gibran, Khalil, "The Prophet," First published by Alfred A Knopf, New York USA in 1923.

Hesse, Hermann, "Siddhartha," Published by New Directions USA, 1922 and 1951.

Naima, Mikhail, "The Book of Mirdad," First published in Lebanon, 1948, later by Watkins Publishing London UK, 2011.

Allen, James, "As a Man Thinketh," First published by Innovative Eggz LLC, USA in 1903, later by L. N. Fowler and Co, London 1911.

Nightingale, Earl, "The Strangest Secret," First was a spoken word record released by Nightingale McHugh Company USA, 1956. Later many editions were published in print by various publishers.

Akerstrom, Lola A, "Lagom: The Swedish Secret of Living Well," Published by Hachette UK, 2017.

Brits, Louisa Thomsen, "The Book of Hygge: The Danish Art of Living Well," Published by Ebury Press and Random House UK, 2016.

Mogi, Ken, "The Little Book of Ikigai: The Secret Japanese way to live a happy life," Published by Quercus Publishing, 2017.

Alborzian, Cameron Yogi, "The Yogi Code: Seven Universal Laws of Infinite Success," Published by Simon and Schuster, 2017.

Vasudev, Jaggi, "Inner Engineering: A Yogi's Guide to Joy," Authored by Sadhguru, an Indian yogi and mystic, Published by Penguin Books and Spiegel & Grau, 2016.

Sri Ramana Maharshi, "Be As You Are," The teachings of Sri Ramana Maharshi compiled and translation by English writer David Godman, Published by Penguin UK, 1988.

Sri Ramana Maharshi, "Who Am I?" Published by CreateSpace Independent Publishing Platform, 2016.

Krishnamurti, Jiddu (1895 – 1986) was a philosopher, speaker and writer. In his early life, he was groomed to be the new world teacher, but later rejected this mantle and said he had no allegiance to any nationality, caste, religion, or philosophy.

Worldhistory.com website, Wikipedia, Inspirational and Moral stories from various sources on world wide web.

www.ingramcontent.com/pod-product-compliance
Lightning Source LLC
Chambersburg PA
CBHW041139110526
44590CB00027B/4068